Wainwright in the Valleys
of Lakeland

Wainwright in the Valleys of Lakeland

With Photographs by Derry Brabbs

Michael Joseph
LONDON

MICHAEL JOSEPH LTD

Published by the Penguin Group
27 Wrights Lane, London W8 5TZ
Viking Penguin Inc., 375 Hudson Street, New York, New York 10014, USA
Penguin Books Australia Ltd, Ringwood, Victoria, Australia
Penguin Books Canada Ltd, 10 Alcorn Avenue, Toronto, Ontario, Canada M4V 3B2
Penguin Books (NZ) Ltd, 182–190 Wairau Road, Auckland 10, New Zealand

Penguin Books Ltd, Registered Offices: Harmondsworth, Middlesex, England

First published in Great Britain September 1992
Second impression September 1993

Typeset in 10 on 12pt Linotron Galliard
by Goodfellow & Egan Phototypesetting Ltd, Cambridge
Colour reproduction by Anglia Graphics Ltd, Bedford
Printed and bound in Italy by L.E.G.O., Vicenza

A CIP catalogue record for this book is available from the British Library

ISBN 0 7181 3481 8

The moral right of the author has been asserted.

Title Page; Left *View across Derwentwater from Castle Head*
Right *Great Crag from Watendlath*
Endpapers *Elterwater*
Page vii *Grasmere from Loughrigg Terrace*

CONTENTS

Also by A. Wainwright and Derry Brabbs

FELLWALKING WITH WAINWRIGHT
WAINWRIGHT ON THE PENNINE WAY
WAINWRIGHT'S COAST TO COAST WALK
WAINWRIGHT IN SCOTLAND
WAINWRIGHT ON THE LAKELAND MOUNTAIN PASSES
WAINWRIGHT'S FAVOURITE LAKELAND MOUNTAINS

By A. Wainwright and Ed Geldard

WAINWRIGHT IN THE LIMESTONE DALES

Pictorial Guides by A. Wainwright
all available from Michael Joseph

Pictorial Guides to the Lakeland Fells

BOOK ONE THE EASTERN FELLS
BOOK TWO THE FAR EASTERN FELLS
BOOK THREE THE CENTRAL FELLS
BOOK FOUR THE SOUTHERN FELLS
BOOK FIVE THE NORTHERN FELLS
BOOK SIX THE NORTH WESTERN FELLS
BOOK SEVEN THE WESTERN FELLS

THE OUTLYING FELLS OF LAKELAND
PENNINE WAY COMPANION
A COAST TO COAST WALK
WALKS IN LIMESTONE COUNTRY
WALKS ON THE HOWGILL FELLS

*The memorial to A. Wainwright in Buttermere Church,
erected by the vicar and the treasurer of the
Parochial Church Council.*

INTRODUCTION

SWAN SONGS OFTEN contain a chord of melancholy. Having to write THE END after a long period of enjoyable experiences evokes sadness. So it is with me. After a post-retirement adopted literary career that has produced seventy books in the past quarter-century, I find myself forced by circumstances to call it a day. Yes, there is sadness but no regrets. This book will be my last. After rather a poor start in life, the world has been very kind to me and, from middle age onwards, everything has gone right. No, no regrets, only gratitude for many blessings.

My eyes, which had served me well for eighty years, began to fail me about four years ago. I became aware of this when I found I began to have difficulty with the small type and symbols of the Ordnance maps, long my favourite reading material, and newspapers, which mattered less. Confirmation of this growing disability was apparent when I climbed Haystacks above Buttermere three years ago. Haystacks was always a favourite fell and I knew its paths well, but on this occasion I slipped and stumbled badly even on familiar ground, not because the rain misted my glasses but because I could not see where I was putting my feet. I knew then that I had come to another THE END. The rain never ceased and Haystacks wept for me that day.

Now I live in a shroud of mist. The world has lost its detail. But in the gathering gloom there is great comfort in closing my eyes and seeing clearly a host of memories, evergreen still, of happy days long gone, and of the beauties and wonders of my beloved country.

I have lived as a semi-recluse over the past few decades, dedicated to my writing, but I have watched events from a distance and I do not like the changes I see in falling standards and values. In the old days, people were grateful for the little they had but it has changed today as people complain and criticise and demand hand-outs as of right. This is a wonderful world, as Louis Armstrong used to tell us, and it would be a lot more wonderful without many of the people now in it. The difference between then and now is that people today collect grouses where formerly they counted their blessings.

I am the last person qualified to preach to others, but I offer to readers three injunctions for their future visits to Lakeland where I hope they will find the pleasures I found: to avoid accidents and always to watch where you are putting your feet; to be kind to animals and respect their dignity; and, third, to stop griping and to count your blessings every night at the close of every day.

From a slippered retirement, goodbye.

AW finished this book at the end of 1990 and this introduction was found in his typewriter, with a cat pawmark or two and a few shreds of baccy, after he died on 20 January 1991.

PART ONE

The Eastern Valleys

High Hartsop Dodd
Left *Longsleddale*

THE VALLEYS OF SHAP FELLS

To THE EAST of the major valleys of Longsleddale and Mardale rises a lofty tract of moorland, a dissected plateau, uninhabited and unfrequented, with several named summits more generally known collectively as Shap Fells. This barren upland, bare of trees and lacking distinctive features, is uninviting and inhospitable. There are few paths and little shelter, and in forty square miles of desolate terrain there is only one recognised crossing: an old packhorse trail long gone to seed. There are few signs of man's intrusion apart from a few decaying boundary walls and fences; true, there are the customary cairns on most of the summits but these were mainly erected by shepherds to provide identifiable landmarks when the fells are shrouded in mist, not by passing walkers.

The landscape is uninspiring, contrasting unfavourably with the exciting array of peaks seen to the west. Although there are few surface indications of human activity, far below ground tunnels pierce the area from end to end, not designed in a quest for mineral wealth but to carry water from Haweswater south to Manchester and places along the way.

Bannisdale from Lamb Crag Pasture

As the central plateau gradually declines to the east and south-east, well-defined ridges spring from it and maintain a high elevation, like fingers spreading from the palm of a hand, and between them the contours relent to form descending and deepening valleys. These carry streams from the silent wilderness above to the pulsating lifeline provided by the A6 highway linking Kendal and Shap; this is a road which climbs to 1390ft and is notorious for winter storms. A lower level and less hazardous alternative is now offered by the M6 motorway a few miles east. For several miles hereabouts, the A6 and the National Park boundary coincide.

The region of Shap Fells is an undisturbed sanctuary for creatures of the wild, provides rough grazing for sheep and fell ponies, and is overflown by curlews, buzzards and the Mardale eagles. This is their country, not man's. Only in the valleys described next are there signs of human occupation past and present.

BANNISDALE

Bannisdale is the shyest of valleys. The issuing stream, Bannisdale Beck, passes under the A6 on its way to join the River Mint but the valley itself is hidden from sight by a screen of trees and is not suspected by travellers on the road. Access to it, as though intended to deter intruders, does not accompany the beck upstream, as is usual, but leaves the A6 a mile south of this point. There a narrow lane without a signpost branches left and almost immediately forks, left to Mosergh Farm and right to Bannisdale, soon reaching the farm buildings of the Old Plough. This short section of the lane overlays the original, very primitive road to Scotland, which was then superseded by a turnpike that subsequently became classified as the A6. In those far-off days, the Old Plough was a place of refreshment but lost patronage when a new Plough Inn was built nearby on the turnpike. At the Old Plough, the mediaeval road, still discernible as a grassy track, crosses fields to Bannisdale High Bridge, now also replaced and bypassed. The road into Bannisdale continues over a low rise and then sharply descends a narrow cutting between high banks, the strip of tarmac being little wider than a car.

It was in this tight defile that, a few years ago, I suffered two minutes of panic amounting to terror. My wife Betty and I were both passengers in a car driven by a friend, and were returning to the A6 after an exploratory visit to the valley. At the bottom of the incline, a farmworker warned us that a herd of cattle was being brought down the road and their arrival was imminent; he advised us to reverse and get out of the way. As there was no sign of them, our friend, not a person who relishes being told what to do, ignored this advice and went on up the road, only to be suddenly halted midway by the appearance of about thirty beasts coming over the rise at the gallop and bearing down on us like a stampede of buffaloes. In a matter of seconds, we were assailed by a heaving, sweating mass of beef on the hoof, frightened at the impasse we were causing as they lurched against the car, frantically struggling to get past in the constricted space available to them. It was a daylight nightmare for the occupants of the car as we were rocked from side to side in a trap: our friend didn't turn a hair, she wouldn't, but my wife and I were palsied by fear. Then, as suddenly, all was quiet as the last of the beasts squeezed past, followed by two sheepdogs who eyed us with looks of admonishment for creating an obstruction to their work. I like cows but not at a distance of inches. They must have sustained superficial injuries from their encounter with an immovable object, but the car was undamaged apart from a few fresh dents and we continued our journey in trembling silence. I rate this my worst experience in fifty years of wandering in Lakeland.

View from Dryhowe Bridge

Upon emerging from the bottom of the cutting, the upper part of the valley is fully revealed as a long trench deeply enclosed between high ridges linked in the far distance by steep slopes descending from the plateau beyond. It is an austere and barren prospect relieved only slightly by the isolated farmsteads of Dry Howe and Bannisdale Head, and offers little inducement to seekers of natural beauty to proceed further. The road turns up the valley to its early terminus at Dryhowe Bridge, a simple span over Bannisdale Beck. Here farm access roads continue, along the west side of the stream to Dry Howe, and across the bridge another leads for two further miles to the buildings of Bannisdale Head. The landscape is bare of trees apart from a few straggling the beckside and a scattered woodland on the breast of the west ridge and although a few walls indicate a limited cultivation, the overriding impression is of primeval and untamed wildness unchanged since the glaciers retreated from the scene.

Bannisdale today is silent, secluded and rarely disturbed by visitors, but there are signs that the valley accommodated a much larger population thousands of years ago, the sites of two ancient settlements having been discovered in the vicinity of Dryhowe Bridge. One, at an elevation on the west side, is listed as Robin Green Dryhowe Pasture and is not easy to reach; the other, Lamb Crag Pasture, is within five minutes' walk of the bridge on the east side and is in the form of a levelled platform with the remains of hut circles enclosed by a parapet.

There was more activity in the valley a few decades ago when Manchester's water engineers exercised their over-developed sixth sense in searching for locations for new reservoirs and sank trial holes near Dryhowe Bridge for a dam, a project happily abandoned. Too long had the lads from south Lancashire been Lakeland's greatest predators. Bannisdale escaped their net.

Below Dryhowe Bridge, the harshness of the valley is softened by a wealth of trees as the beck descends in cascades alongside the ornamental gardens and grounds of Lowbridge House, an attractive residence that seems out of place in so primitive an environment. Built in 1837 and later enlarged, the house was for generations the home of the Fothergill family who maintained a team of horses and a private coach long into the present century. The name of the house refers to Bannisdale Low Bridge which carries the A6. This made virtually obsolete an older bridge, Bannisdale High Bridge, which is upstream across a pretty dell and on the route of the first road over Shap Fells. Beyond the two bridges, the beck hurries down to join the River Mint, and ultimately reaches Morecambe Bay by way of the River Kent.

Bannisdale Head

Upper Borrowdale

BORROWDALE *(in Westmorland)*

Of the streams draining eastwards from the central mass of Shap Fells, the longest and largest is Borrow Beck which occupies the valley that makes the greatest incision in the barren landscape. From a birthplace in a desolation of rank grass and marshes at an altitude of around 1600ft, the infant waters meander slowly across a flat and featureless expanse of moorland, uncertain which way to go and being joined by tributaries similarly initially devoid of a sense of direction. But gradually, after some hesitation, a channel is formed heading south-east, where it is deflected by the contours into a deepening valley ahead. This is Borrowdale, a long trench between confining ridges of lofty elevation, barriers excluding contact with the neighbouring parallel valleys of Bannisdale and Crookdale.

The descending stream, after a few lonely and uneventful miles, reaches lower levels and flows past the only buildings in the upper valley, the farm of Borrowdale Head, and then, as the enclosing ridges decline sufficiently to allow a crossing by vehicular traffic, passes under High Borrow Bridge which was built to carry the original road over Shap summit, a primitive track of cart-width. Some years ago, this section of the old road was surfaced to facilitate the transport of men and materials during the construction of the second Haweswater aqueduct, but has since fallen into virtual disuse again. Packhorse traders travelled this way, then the only western link with Scotland, and it was the route of retreat of Bonnie Prince Charlie's army after their abortive foray into England; a Highlander's purse (empty) was found hereabouts and is now in Kendal Museum.

Beyond the bridge, Borrow Beck is immediately joined by the stream issuing from Crookdale and within a long stone's throw of the confluence their combined waters pass under the A6 at Huck's Bridge where this once-important highway starts a long climb to Shap summit. The A6, having earned an infamous record for accidents and hazardous winter conditions, was in turn superseded in 1970 by the M6 motorway which follows a lower and more sheltered route some miles to the east. Shap summit, since early mediaeval times the busy gateway to the north, has fallen silent and sullen; it is hard to accept redundancy after centuries of service.

Lower Borrowdale

The A6 cuts across the middle of Borrowdale, dividing the valley into two distinct and contrasting parts. The upper is bare and uninviting although within the National Park; the lower, outside the Park, is a gradual transition from austere wildness to more interesting terrain, graced by colour and beauty, and finally ends in a flourish of lovely native woodlands alongside a maturing Borrow Beck. It is a picture of rural tranquillity deep below sheltering ridges. Lower Borrowdale, unknown to tourists, its charms unsuspected, its peace undisturbed, is a hiding place of secret delights.

The way into the lower section of the valley leaves the A6 south of Huck's Bridge near the site of a once-familiar roadside landmark: a large clock supported on an iron framework and standing in isolation for many decades gave the time of day to the numerous travellers on the busy highway. Known as the Leyland clock because of the advertisement it carried, and maintained in working order by the wife of a nearby farmer, this venerable object suffered a deadly blow to its pride when the new motorway took away the traffic and left it deserted and forlorn, offering a service no longer wanted. Sympathisers dismantled, removed and re-erected it in the grounds of the Brewery Arts Centre in Kendal where it enjoys a new lease of life.

From the road a rough track descends to the beck. Walking along here one day about twenty years ago, I was surprised to find a rain gauge recently installed near the path, the significance of which was later revealed by the public announcement of a proposal to construct a reservoir in the valley, a threat of sacrilege subsequently and thankfully abandoned.

The track passes the ruins of High Borrowdale and goes on to reach the only habitation in the lower valley, the still active farm of Low Borrowdale. Here it becomes a rough road and soon crosses the beck at a spacious bathing pool, jealously kept secret by the few local people who have discovered it. Then the road climbs amongst trees to an open heath, a habitat of wild flowers with the purple orchid supreme, and reaches a rustic bridge over a tributary where a tarmac surface gives an easy last mile under a canopy of foliage to the end of the valley – and the end of peace, the song of birds and the murmur of the beck being drowned by the incessant roar of traffic.

Borrowdale surrenders its identity upon entering the Lune Gorge, a spectacular natural defile watered by the River Lune, closely bordered by steep fells, and long acclaimed as the scenic highlight of the southern approach to Scotland. Borrow Beck emerges from quiet seclusion to find, with wide-eyed amazement, a sudden confrontation of noisy commercial turbulence, four bridges in close company spanning its waters before allowing an escape to join the parent river, destiny fulfilled.

Through the ages, the Lune Gorge has offered the only easy passage in a barrier of high and hostile ground, an offer accepted in turn by the early nomadic Britons, the Romans, the packhorse traders, the road makers, the Victorian railway surveyors and recently by the motorway contractors, their lines of communication running side by side in a space so constricted that the road had to be re-aligned to make room for the latest comer. Once silent except for the music of the river, the gorge today is an unceasing cacophony of noise, but not even the many invasions of man can detract from the glory of the natural surroundings.

When the Roman legions extended their invasion and occupation of England to the mountainous north-west during the early centuries AD, they encountered very difficult terrain over which they exercised control by constructing a network of roads to link and supply the forts they built at strategic locations to accommodate the military garrisons. Their surveyors must have whooped with joy upon discovering that the course of the River Lune provided a simple through-route between south and north, and exulted still more on finding within the narrow confines a flat expanse of ground, a rarity in these parts, where Borrowdale joined the main valley. This provided a vantage point ideally situated for the building of a fort to command views of the only three possible approaches.

Upper Borrowdale

Site of the Roman fort at Low Borrow Bridge

The Roman name of the fort is not recorded but became known as Low Borrow Bridge after a road was laid alongside in late mediaeval times and crossed Borrow Beck by a bridge so named. No buildings survive on the site, their stones having been plundered for barns and walls, but the site has otherwise remained undisturbed apart from archaeological digs. It is still possible to make it out, now sandwiched between the railway and the old road. The fort was served by a narrow highway leading to it from the south and this continued north to *Brocavum* (Brougham), and is still distinct on the ground in many sections. Almost certainly there would have been a road link with the nearby fort at *Alauna* (Watercrook) in Kendal, the route followed being a matter of conjecture in the absence of evidence: possibly it was overlaid by the present A685. Another claimant is an old track that enters Borrowdale and climbs to a depression in the west ridge now disfigured by a weird apparition known locally as the Monster. This is a GPO station from which the ridge rises to Whinfell Beacon, one of a series of hilltop sites where alarms of invaders were signalled by the lighting of fires. The beacon at Whinfell has a plantation of trees within easy reach to provide fuel.

11

Crookdale

CROOKDALE

Crookdale is the valley seen by travellers on the long incline of the A6 from Huck's Bridge to Shap summit, but has little to merit a second glance. The issuing stream, Crookdale Beck, rises near the gathering grounds of the neighbouring Borrow Beck but is prevented from joining it initially only by a few feet of higher intervening ground. Thus denied company, the infant stream elects to follow a separate course along a parallel fold in the hills, soon becoming confined between high ridges. This is the valley of Crookdale, so named from its final looping curve to join Borrowdale when the dividing ridge sharply declines and ends.

Access to Crookdale is provided by a no-through road, unsignposted, branching from the A6 south of Huck's Bridge. This rises over a spur of land and then falls to High Borrow Bridge, and continues for a mile to end at Hause Foot. This farm building which had been derelict for many years has recently been restored and is again occupied. It is the only habitation in the valley which, from this point upstream, is pathless and unfrequented and is better left to creatures with webbed feet since the beck fails in its efforts to drain the valley floor, turning it into an extensive swamp. Crookdale is the wettest valley underfoot I have ever encountered, but after two miles of floundering, relief can be gained by scrambling up to the west ridge which, in comparison, offers a pleasant return route. It passes over the three summits of Lord's Seat, Robin Hood and High House Bank before descending to the access road.

Crookdale Bridge and Hause Foot   Below *Old road to Crookdale from Upper Borrowdale*

The silence and seclusion of Crookdale were disturbed by a spasm of activity some years ago when the second Haweswater aqueduct emerged from its tunnel under the fells in the rough pasture near Hause Foot and was continued as a pipeline to the treatment plant at Watchgate, the work being facilitated by laying a surface of tarmac over the original mediaeval road to the far north.

Although Crookdale has little to enthuse walkers, those with an interest in days gone by will find a mild excitement in following the old road in the section between Crookdale Bridge and Wasdale Old Bridge which has many relics of the past. The old road climbs the steep fellside behind Hause Foot, and is still mostly distinct and retains its original culverts. It is crossed by the A6 just beyond the summit, and continues thence around the far side of Packhorse Hill to Wasdale Beck, passing on its way an ancient milestone (Shap 6, Kendal 10) and the ruins of an inn (named Demmings on a map dated 1770).

WASDALE *(in Westmorland)*

Mecca, for fellwalkers in Lakeland, is the valley of Wasdale in the south-west of the district, the birthplace of the sport of rock-climbing in England, with an associated history of legend and literature and high adventure. A popular centre for mountain expeditions in scenes of unsurpassed natural grandeur, a magnet that draws admirers and turns them into addicts. That Wasdale has an air of magic.

But there is another Wasdale, also within the National Park, that few have heard of and fewer still visited. And, truth to tell, they have no cause for regret. This Wasdale has no charms, no inducements, no friends; the derelict farm buildings of Wasdale Head emphasise only neglect and a hopeless abandonment. The valley comes alongside the A6 north of the road summit and is seen by all travellers on that highway but offers nothing to invite even a temporary halt. It is usually passed unnoticed, a roadside planting of conifers partly obstructing the view. The one feature hereabouts that does catch the eye and cannot be ignored is the immense Shap Granite Quarry which, after many years of exploitation, has carved a huge slice out of the fellside forming the northern boundary of the valley. Access to the quarry is by a rough road leaving the A6 and this may be followed further, although now disused, to the ruined farm buildings; otherwise, the valley is without tracks other than those made by sheep. Wasdale has become a no-man's-land.

Ruins of Wasdale Head

Shap Granite Quarry

The valley is closed by a nearby background of fells, of which Great Yarlside is the highest at 1986ft. The Ordnance Survey have been here, but instead of building their customary triangulation column, have been content to embed a circular metal plate in the ground of the summit, this being one of only two such devices in the district; the other is on Seat Robert above Swindale.

Another feature worthy of mention only because the Ordnance Survey have misinterpreted the local dialect, as in other instances, is the naming of a large boulder perched on a massive plinth of pink granite as: 'To Stone or to'ther' on the large-scale maps instead of the more likely 'Top stone on t'other'.

Wasdale Beck adds a sparkle of life to a deserted landscape as it flows down the valley from Great Yarlside below the ruined farm buildings and passes under the A6, here leaving the National Park, then under Wasdale Old Bridge near an ancient long barrow that has insensitively been planted with spruce. The stream heads north-east as though destined for the River Eden but changes both name and direction, turning south in a wide loop to join the River Lune near Tebay. Thus it disproves what appears to be the obvious fact that Shap summit is the main watershed between north and south: the true watershed is further north beyond Shap Wells Hotel.

WET SLEDDALE

Wet Sleddale was the last victim of Manchester's insatiable thirst for Lakeland's water and in this quiet valley of scattered farmsteads are the inevitable consequences of abandoned buildings, tumbled walls and drowned pastures. A massive dam and a reservoir to augment Haweswater have radically transformed the appearance and character of this peaceful hollow amongst the hills, and although Manchester has tried to salve its conscience by making a tarred road to the dam and a car park (more, one suspects, for their own use rather than that of visitors) and has re-sited and rebuilt an old bridge engulfed by the flood, the silence is not of peace but of death.

Wet Sleddale is wide and less encompassed by high ground than the other valleys in the Shap Fells. Except for an ancient packhorse trail coming over from Longsleddale, the surrounding heights carry no paths and retain their pristine wildness. There is a track from the valley up the hillside to a shooting hut on the south side and this may be used as a springboard for a circuit of the horseshoe ridges, joining and returning by the packhorse trail which is still distinct and becomes tarred in its later stages to serve the few farms. Where the trail reaches the valley, a Victorian postbox set in a roadside wall is still used by the little community. Sleddale Beck, in a pleasant fringe of trees, drains the upper reaches of the valley and enters the reservoir, issuing therefrom as the River Lowther; in times of heavy rain, it comes over the spillway like a miniature Niagara. The Lowther soon turns north into a valley of its own choosing, passing the ruins of Shap Abbey and the grounds of Lowther Castle on a pleasant journey to the River Eamont.

Road access to Wet Sleddale is from the A6 south of Shap village. From this entrance, a private waterworks road branches off to cross open fells to Swindale and Haweswater.

The reservoir at Wet Sleddale

Wet Sleddale

One feature in the valley, unique in Lakeland, is a mediaeval deer trap, no longer in use but well preserved. This is found by continuing on foot from the car park along a track on the south side of the reservoir, passing the new bridge spanning the inflowing Sleddale Beck, to an arrangement of walls about ten or twelve feet high which enclose a green sward with only one entrance. This was built by the early settlers as a living larder for replenishment of their food supplies. The deer have gone from the valley, but happily settled in the open pastures below the dam is a considerable colony of fell ponies. Not all living creatures have deserted Wet Sleddale; some, two-legged and four-legged, love it still. The four-legged, undisturbed, think it heaven.

Fell ponies in Wet Sleddale

Swindale

SWINDALE

Swindale follows a parallel course to the neighbouring valley of Mardale, a high ridge forming a barrier between them, but although inhabited it is little known. The one road access is remote from the usual tourist routes, branching without a flourish of signposts from the bottom road between Rosgill and Bampton. Swindale may almost be described as a secret valley. Lacking an inn or shop or a church, it has no attraction for visitors wishing to spend money; the amenities, all free, are provided by nature.

The lower reaches of the valley are crossed in a great loop by a private waterworks road linking Wet Sleddale and Haweswater and available for use by local farmers. Manchester's water engineers, ever on the lookout for liquid supplies, were quick to locate Swindale and plunder the valley stream, Swindale Beck, but to their credit did so unobtrusively.

Swindale is a narrow fold in the fells, deeply enclosed towards its head by high ground of which Selside Pike is the dominant summit. Its stream comes sharply down from an unseen upland depression, Mosedale, and retains the name of Mosedale Beck on the descent but changes to Swindale Beck upon reaching the valley. On this stream, nearing the foot of the slope, is a tumble of waterfalls, the Forces, adding sparkle to a drab landscape. Also leaving Mosedale and accompanying the stream down to Swindale is an old path which was probably first used by men employed at the vast Mosedale Quarry until work there ceased; this enters a lane down in the valley and proceeds to the first buildings at Swindale Head, the terminus of a tarred road through the valley. A few roadside farms and a modest waterworks complex follow as the tarmac strip rises to cross the private Haweswater road before descending to the public highway near Rosgill.

A notable feature seen when passing along the valley is the long cliff of Gouther Crag fringing the eastern skyline: this is the one harsh aspect in a peaceful scene where green pastures and woodlands blend in perfect harmony against a dark background of sombre fells, an air of quiet contentment pervading all.

18

Swindale, where nothing of general interest ever earns headlines, nevertheless has a place in local history. Before 1729, when the precincts of the church at Mardale Green were first consecrated for burials, the dead of that little community were conveyed, strapped on the backs of horses, for internment at Shap, eight miles distant across high and lonely fells. The route followed climbs steeply from Mardale Green in a series of zigzags to ease the gradient (this section now being interrupted by the new tarmac road to Mardale Head), traverses Mardale Common at an elevation of around 1700ft and then declines to Swindale Head, there turning down the valley to a bridge giving access to a long incline around the facing fells. It finally descends gradually to a crossing of the River Lowther and an uphill mile to Shap. The route of these melancholy cortèges was known as the Corpse Road. It is still fairly distinct on the ground, the later stages having been overlaid by tarmac roads. Sad associations forgotten, the Old Corpse Road now provides a good walk for the living.

Below *Near Swindale Head*   Above *The Forces*

THE LOWTHER VALLEY

THE RIVER LOWTHER issues from Wet Sleddale and at the first opportunity allowed by the contours turns north into a more fertile valley and gentler surroundings, flowing along a green strath in leisurely loops as though loth to leave this pleasant arcadia. The valley is wide and is confined, not too closely, between foothills rising in the west to the skyline of the High Street range and, in the east, the limestone cliffs of Knipe Scar which borders on the vast estate of Lowther Park. Knipe Scar has a stone circle and other antiquities on its crest.

Attractive villages and settlements are spaced along the course of the river, and nearby. First met, travelling downriver, is Keld, as old as its name, with a humble sixteenth-century chapel now in the care of the National Trust, and this is succeeded on the opposite bank by the venerable ruins of Shap Abbey.

The history of Shap Abbey began in 1191 with the foundation at Preston Patrick near Kendal of a convent for Premonstratensian canons, this establishment being moved to Shap in 1201 when construction of the abbey was commenced. Work continued on various additions into the sixteenth century. In 1540 it was surrendered to Henry VIII and then fell into disrepair and ruin, many of the carved stones being moved to Lowther Castle. Early this century, the structure was in a bad state but happily was taken over by the Ministry of Works in 1948 and further decay has been arrested by a consolidation of all the remaining fabric, of which only the west tower retains its original height. It is preserved as an ancient monument and access by the public is permitted.

A captive sheep is given the duty of keeping the grass cropped, a task it performs well and with obvious pleasure.

The early ecclesiastics selected the sites of their ministrations with care, beauty of environs and a neighbouring river being prerequisites, and Shap Abbey conforms to pattern: the setting is delightful, and after eight hundred years there is still a pervading peace and a mystical magic in this hallowed ground.

Beyond Shap Abbey, the river arrives at Rosgill Bridge, this carrying a quiet road linking the hillside village of Rosgill and the valley settlements of Bampton and Bampton Grange. These have all been given a new lease of life by the recent demand for cottages in the country.

A conspicuous obelisk on the limestone heights above Rosgill has the name of Mary's Pillar. It was erected in 1854 by a local man as a memorial to his daughter, Mary, who died at the age of twenty-four.

Shap Abbey

20

The two Bamptons are rather superior, having between them a river bridge and a handsome church (St Patrick's), an inn and a meeting of roads, one of which is the key to Haweswater and Mardale. Bampton stakes a claim to be regarded as the capital of the upper part of the valley.

A mile further, the shy hamlet of Butterwick stands back from the road as if hoping to be passed unnoticed. The buildings here border a stream, crossed by a stone footbridge, on its way to join the river. The next tributary, passing under the road at Beckfoot Bridge, is Heltondale Beck. Then the village of Helton is reached, or may be bypassed, the road continuing to Askham where it is joined by another that has followed a parallel course on the east side of the river along the boundary of Lowther Park and serving the immaculate estate cottages of Knipe and Whale.

Until 1974, when Askham was within Westmorland, the consensus, rarely questioned or disputed, was that it was the prettiest village in that county. Westmorland is officially no more but Askham remains to delight visitors with charming cottages, ample verges and graceful trees preserving its enviable distinction. The nearness of the lovely river and the stately environs of Lowther Castle add prestige to beauty.

Above *Mary's Pillar*
Below *Askham*

Lowther Castle

From a crossroads the main street, a pleasant avenue, goes down to the river, passing on the left the grounds of Askham Hall, the residence of the present Earl of Lonsdale: this was the ancient manor house of the estate, first occupied in 1375. Adjoining the river bridge is the church of St Peter (formerly St Columba); it was rebuilt in 1838 by the architect who designed Lowther Castle. Over the bridge, the road enters the spacious grounds of the castle.

Lowther Castle, for long the family seat of the Earls of Lonsdale, occupies the site of mansions dating back to the reign of Edward I, all traces of these early residences being destroyed in a disastrous fire in 1726 that left the place in ruins. In 1802, work commenced on the building of the castle, commissioned by the second Earl to a design in various styles of architecture that gave an effect of elegance and strength. The castle earned renown for its wide sphere of activities and the entertainment of distinguished guests, especially during the life of the fifth Earl, a man with many sporting associations, a friend of royalty and a national figure of great influence and authority still fresh in the memory.

Sadly, following the death of the fifth Earl Lonsdale, the castle was abandoned, the interior dismantled and gutted and only the walls left standing as a spectacular memorial to past glories.

Lowther church and mausoleum

The spacious grounds of Lowther Park are entirely delightful, magnificent avenues of noble trees adding grace and dignity to beautiful vistas of landscaped gardens. A public road crosses the estate, giving easy access to the parish church of St Michael which still preserves a twelfth-century arcade, twice greatly altered, and an interior with many tombs, effigies and monuments. In the churchyard is a private mausoleum; built in 1857, it contains a fine marble statue and sarcophagus of William, second Earl of Lonsdale, who died in 1832. Neat estate houses, nicely arranged and spaced, and tenanted by local people who take a pride in their environment and care for it, contribute to the well-being and contentment of the little community. The beauty and serenity of Lowther are a tonic to jaded urban dwellers.

In 1969 an area in Lowther Park was opened to the public as a wildlife reserve and proved to be very popular. As well as many species of deer, cattle and sheep, a variety of exotic birds and wild animals in enclosures could be seen. Visitors were appreciative, but not everybody enthuses about the caging of wild animals: to these animals liberty is life, and the instinct for freedom is not curbed by regular feeding. I am glad that Lowther Park now concentrates on leisure activities for its visitors.

Beyond Lowther Park, the river passes out of the National Park and joins the Eamont.

Heltondale

HELTONDALE

Few visitors to Lakeland have heard of Heltondale or found the name on maps of the district and fewer still have been there in the absence of inducements to do so. In an area internationally renowned for the loveliness of its valleys, Heltondale is a poor relation, and aware of it, concentrating on farming and not on catering for tourists. The valley lacks not only the charm of others but their usual configuration, this being like a great hollow scooped out of the fellside of Loadpot Hill at the northern extremity of the High Street range and giving allegiance exclusively to the Lowther domain. Streams unite to form Heltondale Beck, this being plundered to supply the Haweswater reservoir by an aqueduct, the escaping flow joining the River Lowther. A minor road curves round the hollow, linking Helton and Bampton by a roundabout route designed to serve the farms and not the care of strangers.

Starting from Helton, this road leaves the main street and climbs to open country where the cars of family parties often assemble on the unenclosed verges for the flying of kites and other innocent pastimes. A track leaves here to cross Moor Divock, a place to gladden the eyes of antiquarians since there is a stone circle, a Roman road, and many tumuli and standing stones within easy reach. The road becomes a bridleway and goes on in a wide sweep around the hollow before finally turning down to Bampton.

Heltondale is not a place that lingers in the memory.

MARDALE

UNTIL SIXTY YEARS ago, Haweswater in Mardale was the shy Cinderella of the lakes, rarely visited, the only road access being little better than a country lane. She had no suitors among the Lake Poets, and was deeply conscious that, in popular esteem, she was considered very inferior to her big sisters, Windermere and Ullswater. When a Prince did finally come to claim her affection he was not a Prince Charming but an arrogant and ambitious overlord with grand plans for transforming her modest dimensions into a vast expanse of water that would occupy the whole valley, just as he had done at Thirlmere half a century earlier. It was a pity, he admitted, that his scheme would involve the displacement of the dalesfolk living in the valley but, he argued, he was prompted only by an intention to serve the common good and the changes he proposed would be of benefit to a greater number. His name was Manchester Corporation.

So the rape of Mardale proceeded. A massive dam was constructed and, as the water level rose, the little beaches of shingle where the cows loved to stand were soon submerged. In due course, the primitive lane which had served the doomed hamlet of Mardale Green at the head of the valley was drowned. In deference to the ensuing outcry, a road was made along the eastern side above the hotel which was built to replace the centuries-old Dun Bull at Mardale Green.

Access to Mardale is from either Bampton or Bampton Grange and a signposted country lane heads south in the near company of Haweswater Beck on its way to join the river after its discharge from the reservoir dam. Within a mile there is a glimpse of Thornthwaite Hall on the left: this was built as the family home of the Curwens in the sixteenth century, and is now bereft of its original embattled pele tower and is occupied as a farmhouse. Beyond, the road forks, giving alternative routes to Mardale Head, the one chosen depending on the means of locomotion: motorists must branch left while walkers can continue forward to Burn Banks to start a four-mile marathon along the west side.

Haweswater Reservoir today and, right, *before its conversion in the late 1930s. The thick black line indicates the water level of the reservoir.*

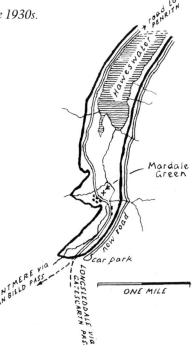

The motor road descends to a bridge over Haweswater Beck and then rises gently to come abreast of the dam. On the way, it passes the junction with the private waterworks road from Wet Sleddale, constructed to give a quicker approach to Haweswater from the south. Also joining here is the access lane to Naddle House, a farmstead isolated in the heart of Naddle Forest, a large native wood of oak and sycamore, beech and elm that puts to shame the massed conifer plantations so much in favour today. Coming down here from an upland wealth of timber is Naddle Beck, avoiding incarceration in the reservoir by preferring to unite with the outflow.

The road beyond the dam is flanked by the reservoir wall, over which can be seen the long skyline of the High Street range and the descending watercourses of Whelter Beck and Measand Beck, both distinguished by waterfalls; on the left of the road rise the steep wooded slopes of Naddle Forest. After two pleasant miles, the Haweswater Hotel is reached: this handsome building, rather grander in style than the native architecture, was erected by Manchester Corporation to replace the doomed Dun Bull. It is now the sole provider of beds and breakfasts for visitors to the valley and is not particularly convenient for those who come by foot. Beyond the hotel, the curving road reveals the impressive head of the valley set deep amongst encircling fells. It is a scene of wild grandeur second in the district only to Wasdale Head: Branstree plunges down on the left, Harter Fell is directly ahead and the descending ridges of High Street are on the right; finally the sharp peak of Kidsty Pike is prominent on the skyline. It is a scene that has increasingly attracted the attention of fellwalkers since the road and its terminal car park provided a springboard for their expeditions.

Mardale from Bampton Common

The road's end at Mardale Head

The Dun Bull at Mardale Green was the social centre of the little community, a meeting place for the local farmers and shepherds, and a welcome halt for walkers entering the valley from the fells above. The church was dismantled in 1936, the stones being used in the construction of the reservoir; the coffins were exhumed and re-buried in a separate cemetery at Shap. This brought events full circle since, before 1729 when the precincts were first consecrated for burial, the dead of Mardale Green were strapped to the backs of horses and taken for internment at Shap along the route known as the Corpse Road. As the journey up the valley proceeds, a wayside signpost points to the Corpse Road which zigzags up the fellside. The next feature to catch the attention is Hopgill Beck, descending on the left in silver cascades from the hinterland of Branstree to add its contribution to the reservoir.

In another half-mile, the end of the road is reached and parking space for cars has been provided but is still often very congested. This is a wonderful place for appraising the ramifications of the valley's head and a wide choice of fellwalking expeditions is available from the car park.

Gatesgarth Pass from Longsleddale and Nan Bield Pass from Kentmere may be combined in a splendid circular walk, their tops linked by a traverse over the summit of Harter Fell which thrusts into the sky between them and from where there is a classic full-length aerial view of Haweswater. Harter Fell dominates the head of the valley, its craggy façade split by deep gullies prohibiting direct access by other than expert climbers. The impregnable appearance of this rocky bastion attracted the golden eagles on their recent return to Lakeland after an absence of 150 years. They have now established a permanent home in the greater seclusion of Riggindale, a mile away.

Two shorter excursions from the car park are especially rewarding: one adopts the Nan Bield path for a visit to Small Water, and the other recommended route leads to Blea Water. Best of all, however, is the ascent to High Street.

Left *The Forces, Measand Beck*   *The ruins of Mardale Green seen when the reservoir waters were very low*

Visitors entering Mardale from Bampton in the north and wishing to reach the head of the valley under their own steam rather than be carried there on wheels should leave the motor road at its junction with Burn Banks and go forward into this sequestered settlement. It was the base of operations for the hundreds of workmen engaged in the construction of the Haweswater dam, and is in a setting so richly timbered that it is better described as a woodland village than as a waterworks encampment. In pre-reservoir times, the valley road continued from Burn Banks to Mardale Green but this was submerged by the rising waters, its loss being compensated by a footpath made at a higher level above the western shore.

Before starting the journey, the dam may be seen at close quarters along a lane rising to the parapet and its massive proportions appreciated. Measuring 1550 feet in length and 90 feet in height, the structure is impressive, even awe-inspiring; it has the further distinction of being the first hollow buttress dam in the world. The water level of the natural lake was raised by 96 feet, doubling its length and trebling its surface area. From the parapet, tunnelled supplies can be seen coming in from Heltondale and Swindale, the storage capacity being the greatest of all reservoirs in the north-west.

The footpath to Mardale Head leaves Burn Banks and climbs towards Bampton Common, turning left along the top of a plantation and then descending to Measand where a large house, a school and a bridge were early victims of the engulfing waters; the site is now submerged but can be identified by the tumbling cascades and waterfalls of Measand Beck. These are known as the Forces and were a popular resort of picnic parties in the old days.

Castle Crag across Haweswater

The path continues along the side of the reservoir and in two further miles crosses Whelter Beck which issues from a vast hollow rimmed by crags in which the eagles have shown interest as a possible second home. Beyond, the path is encroached upon by bracken as it passes below the rocky height of Castle Crag, on the crest of which is Mardale's most ancient relic. This is a British hill fort, hidden from sight below but attainable by a steep scramble; tumbled walls and defensive ditches are all that remains, the best reward for the effort of the climb being the commanding view of the full length of Haweswater cradled in the surrounding fells. Back along the path, the steep slopes on the right relax to reveal the side valley of Riggindale.

RIGGINDALE

Riggindale is a deep trench descending steeply from the rim of the High Street range. Its slopes are littered by rocky debris fallen from an encircling skyline of crags in a scene of desolation presided over by the sharp upthrust of Kidsty Pike. The valley is drained by Riggindale Beck, a feeder of Haweswater. Formerly it had a single habitation, Riggindale Farm, near its outlet and not far from Mardale Green, but this too was sacrificed to the greater needs of Manchester, the deserted pastures becoming a sanctuary for red deer coming over from Martindale, half-wild fell ponies and the ubiquitous foxes.

Then, out of the blue, came a pair of golden eagles, prospecting for a secure location for an eyrie, and finding a site that has served them well for the past two decades. Their coming activated a renewal of human interest in the valley, and voluntary wardens of the Royal Society for the Protection of Birds have established a colony of huts within sight of the nest, their dedicated mission being to keep watchful observance on the movements of the birds and to deter intruders. Visitors with a genuine interest are welcome at the huts, a privilege not accorded to others who might cause disturbance. Even as I write these lines (6 April 1990) the radio announces that two eggs have been laid in the eyrie. There will be rejoicing in Riggindale today.

The first recorded visitor to Riggindale was Hugh Holme who was involved in a conspiracy against King John in the year 1208 and fled north, intending to seek refuge in Scotland. His journey ended when he discovered a cave amongst the crags of Riggindale that offered shelter for himself and his family, and this temporary lodging is still known as Hugh's Cave. He travelled no further north; the remoteness and seclusion of the area were to his liking and he settled permanently in Mardale where he was succeeded by generations of descendants, and acquired such influence and authority in local affairs that he earned the title of 'King of Mardale'.

The present Kings of Mardale are the golden eagles.

Riggindale: the RSPB hut seen in the centre

Haweswater from Mardale Head

THE PATH NOW crosses the outlet of Riggindale and rises gently to the grassy saddle above the trees of The Rigg. This was the site first proposed for a hotel to replace the Dun Bull, a location convenient for walkers, but the needs of motorists were given prior consideration and so the new Haweswater Hotel was built across the water with the advantage of road access.

From The Rigg, the path follows the reservoir wall round to the car park where, unless a departing motorist offers a lift, two miles of tarmac must be trudged to the hotel and a further five miles to Bampton and its infrequent bus service.

Bampton Grange

LONGSLEDDALE

TRAVELLERS HEADING NORTH out of Kendal along the A6 soon leave the urban environment behind and enter open country with a distant prospect of the Lakeland mountains. After four miles, with a growing awareness that the pastoral scene is being succeeded by rougher uplands, a narrow road branches down on the left into Longsleddale and immediately beyond there is a view of the valley, seen full length and at a lower level, which presents a picture of such loveliness that most passersby are halted in their tracks. Revealed at this point is a patchwork of fields and copses, with a scattering of farmhouses along a green ribbon enclosed by shaggy fells and encircled at the far end by greater heights; and, over all, there is a pervading air of rural serenity.

Leaving the A6, the branch road descends sharply to the floor of the valley where it makes acquaintance with the River Sprint at the hamlet of Garnett Bridge. Here there was an eighteenth-century corn mill, one of nine water-powered mills along the course of the river; all are now disused, this one closing in the 1920s.

Garnett Bridge

33

Nearby on the fellside is the filtering plant of the first Haweswater aqueduct, a conspicuous reminder of a traumatic few years in Longsleddale's history. In the 1940s, the peace of the valley was disturbed as it was tunnelled into and cut into to provide a passage for supplies of water from the new reservoir in Mardale. It was Longsleddale's double misfortune to lie on a direct course between Haweswater and Manchester and to have descending contours that enabled the water to flow under its own pressure without the need for pumping; a decided economy. Nature, as always, has proved a great healer and the scars of this nine-mile laceration have gone. Thirty years later, when Manchester proposed a second aqueduct alongside to meet increasing demand, spirited opposition by the dalesfolk thwarted the plan and the second aqueduct was finally laid under Shap Fells a few miles to the east, the flow there being impelled not by gravity but by pumping. And Manchester learned that the people of Longsleddale were proud of their valley. One mutilation was enough.

Beyond Garnett Bridge, the road continues pleasantly up the valley past a few modern bungalows with the river away on the left and a rising fellside on the right. Occasional more mature properties are seen as the journey proceeds, age having added a mellow charm to their stones and sheltering trees a verdant frame.

A lane goes down to the left to cross the river at Nether House Bridge, a seventeenth-century structure built for the passage of packhorses but later widened to admit vehicles to the farms along the west bank of the river; these are all linked by the old and original road up the valley before the present motor road was made along the east side. No packhorses travel it now, and few cars, but there is an infrequent flurry of activity as motor cyclists assemble on the fellside behind Wad's Howe. The old road emerges from a historical past after three pleasant miles, returning to the motor road near the end of the tarmac at Sadgill Bridge.

Longsleddale from near Nether House Bridge

Longsleddale from Ubarrow Hall

The tarmac road goes forward after the branch to Nether House Bridge and passes the oldest habitation in the valley, Ubarrow Hall, which recent occupiers have preferred to name Yewbarrow Hall. This dates from mediaeval times and originally had a pele tower; this has been reduced in height and gabled but retains walls six feet thick, a splendid basement now used as a dairy, and an interior staircase.

The parish church of Longsleddale, dedicated to St Mary, is conveniently sited at mid-point in the valley alongside the road. It was a chapel of Kendal until it was rebuilt in 1712, when it was given parochial status; the present church is the result of a further rebuilding in 1863. Some of the features of the previous churches have been preserved, notably a carved oak door dated 1662 and a silver chalice dated 1577. Church and precincts are on a modest scale, in keeping with the characteristics of the valley.

There is nothing pretentious about Longsleddale except its landscape.

Sadgill Bridge

Past the church, there is a more open aspect ahead as trees give place to pastures, and the head of the valley, now seen at closer range, is revealed as a scene of wild grandeur, a landscape that quickens the pulses with a promise of adventure in high places. A lane crosses the valley floor to Wad's Howe but the lane goes eagerly forward, narrowly constricted by stone walls that defy and deny speeding. On the right, Capplebarrow rises to a height of 1683ft, its easier lower slopes occupied by a string of farms, and then, after passing the entrance to the side valley of Stockdale (*see* page 39), a final stage, here joined by the old road from across the river, ends at Sadgill Bridge in a setting of scenic drama.

Sadgill Bridge is a compulsory halt. Cars can go no further and travellers on foot intending to press on to the upper limits of the valley stop here to check supplies and gird up their loins before venturing into the grim recesses now immediately ahead; if prone to accidents, they should bear in mind that the farm across the bridge is a Mountain Rescue Post.

The view from the bridge is posed perfectly for the camera and inspires a closer approach. The river is seen coming down a rocky defile between the twin portals of Goat Scar and Buckbarrow Crag, with Harter Fell a sombre background: it is an impressive scene that is increasingly attracting the attention of visitors. Times without number in the past I have walked the length of Longsleddale, there being no public bus service, often without meeting a soul, but those days are gone for ever. Sadgill, like so many places in Lakeland, is suffering from overkill. On most fine days, there is severe congestion at the road end caused by the parking of cars, much to the frustration of the residents across the bridge, and although I regard all car parks as blemishes, especially ugly in open country, there really is a need for one here. Sadgill is no longer known only to a few. It is becoming a weekend metropolis.

Goat Scar

From the terminus of the tarred road at Sadgill Bridge, a rough lane continues to the head of the valley, rising sharply at first but soon levelling out along the fellside between walls. This was the route of the packhorse traders, later adopted and improved to give access to the huge Wrengill Quarry ahead. Below, on the left, there is a hiatus in the swift movement of the River Sprint as it meanders through pastures, this being the site of a reservoir planned in 1845 to regulate supplies to the many water-powered mills lower down the valley. But, although authorised by Act of Parliament, the scheme never came to pass, mainly because of the exorbitant cost of a similar undertaking in the neighbouring Kentmere valley. Of interest and still to be seen is a wall built as a dam to prevent debris brought down by the river from spilling over the fields.

As the track starts to climb steeply on its final stage to the quarry, the surroundings become hostile, Goat Scar towering high on the left. This is succeeded by the gloomy hollow of Settle Earth, a refuge for foxes, below the skyline of Kentmere Pike. Even more intimidating are, on the right, the gaunt cliffs of Buckbarrow Crag, a resort of rockclimbers, rising out of a petrified desert of fallen boulders, one of which is reputed to rival the dimensions of the famous Bowder Stone in Borrowdale. Of more immediate interest is the paving of the track on the steepest sections, the stones being laid laterally in courses from side to side to serve as brakes for horses descending with laden sleds and to give them a more secure footing.

In the awesome silence of these barren surroundings only the river, here a chattering infant, has life and movement as it leaps in cascades and waterfalls alongside the track, glad to escape from a tormented passage through the quarry.

Wrengill Quarry

I was here one Sunday morning when I met a rare character, a farmer with compassion for foxes, watching his dogs as they raced up the fellside, on his instructions, in the shadows of Settle Earth. He wanted to talk and told me he had heard there was to be a fox-shoot in the afternoon. He was a supporter of fox-hunting, which offered a chance of escape and instant death if caught, but he deplored the shooting of them which often left them maimed, unable to fend for themselves, and a lingering death from starvation. His purpose that day was to drive the foxes in Settle Earth over the fells into the safety of Mardale.

When the gradient of the track eases at a cross-gate, the wall on the right turns away to make a beeline for the summit of Tarn Crag, the left wall continuing. And over it is Wrengill Quarry, a place for explorers.

Present access to Wrengill Quarry is for walkers only, a stile over the wall being provided. The quarry was last worked by prisoners during the First World War and since their departure it has not been used. Seventy years of decay have robbed it of many surface features, notably a row of cottages, an engine shed and a light railway, but enough remains to interest an industrial archaeologist with an imaginative mind.

Wren Gill comes down from Harter Fell to enter the quarry as a graceful waterfall, disappearing at once into potholes and is thence conducted in underground culverts to its point of debouchure, emerging as the River Sprint. Adits and tunnels are still to be seen in the cliff faces but are probably in a state of collapse and should not be entered.

There is no beauty in this silent and oppressive graveyard of enterprise and endeavour. Yet, walking one day along the top of the cliffs amid scenes of death and devastation, I found a spark of life in the form of a purple carpet of thyme, a sight so lovely that, against my better instincts, I dug up a few roots and took them back to plant in my garden. But they were sad exiles. They did not take kindly to suburbia and soon died. Home for them was Wrengill Quarry and there was no place like it.

Opposite the quarry a fading path turns east into Mosedale which, despite its name, does not measure up to my definition of a valley, being rather an upland depression. Here too is an immense disused quarry, the only other feature of note being a cottage used as an overnight lodging by shepherds. The main path continues beyond the stile into Wrengill Quarry and mounts the slope ahead, zigzags engineered to ease the passage of the packhorses in times long past, to reach the watershed of Gatesgarth Pass, crossed by a boundary fence that marks the beginning of Mardale and the end of Longsleddale.

STOCKDALE

The entrance to the side valley of Stockdale is passed on the journey up Longsleddale half a mile short of Sadgill, a lane leading into it to serve the solitary habitation of Stockdale Farm but going no further, nor are there any footpaths beyond. This unfrequented breach in the fells is closed at its head by Grey Crag which sends down two tributaries to the main drain, Stockdale Beck, a feeder of the River Sprint. The privacy of this quiet recess was cruelly disturbed fifty years ago when the Haweswater aqueduct was laid across it, here surfacing to daylight after a five-mile underground passage below the watershed. A relic of this undertaking is seen on Great Howe, high above the west flank of the valley: here stands one of three survey posts indicating the line of the aqueduct hundreds of feet below, the others being on Branstree and Tarn Crag. Except for the collapse of a wooden platform on Tarn Crag, all have survived the elements well and no doubt will be objects of curious speculation in years to come.

Stockdale

KENTMERE

KENTMERE IS AN unusual name for a valley, and is taken from a small and shallow lake formed and fed by the River Kent during its passage from the slopes of High Street to Morecambe Bay. The lake was drained in the mid-nineteenth century, coincidental with the construction of a reservoir higher in the valley. The object of reclaiming more land for grazing was not entirely successful, the site of the lake remaining very marshy. The name, however, had already been adopted for the valley and a nearby village.

There is only one access by road into the valley, this leaving the industrial village of Staveley, recently bypassed, on the busy approach to Windermere. After suffering the turbulence and congestion of traffic for decades, Staveley has recovered much of its former quiet attractiveness. Here the Kent is joined by the River Gowan and its resident colony of mallard ducks in a pleasant setting backed by low fells. The main street, with more breathing space, has a few shops and the clock tower of St Margaret's Church, preserved when the body of the church was demolished in 1865 and replaced by another, St James's, off the Kentmere road.

The weir at Barley Bridge

Kentmere from near Scroggs Bridge

The road into Kentmere leaves the village centre unobtrusively and is now more likely than ever to go unnoticed as the bypass deflects cars heading eagerly for Windermere and places beyond. Moreover, it is not a through route, coming to a dead end with no alternative return and therefore has little appeal to touring motorists. Nor has the highway authority effected improvements by widening and cutting corners. Consequently, and happily, the valley remains relatively quiet, unspoiled and undisturbed. Leaving the village, the road passes between the church and a small factory to reach Barley Bridge; this is not crossed but deserves a halt to see the curving weir, a sickle of leaping white water, a spectacular foreground to a vista of open country ahead.

Past Barley Bridge, the valley takes shape, narrowing between rising fellsides and the prospect ahead holds a promise, soon to be fulfilled, of increasing loveliness. Scroggs Bridge, next reached, spans the lively river as it emerges from a background of trees, and is a prelude to enchanting scenes to follow. Here the main valley road crosses to the east bank but a minor one goes forward along the west side, rounding Hugill Fell, which has on its crest the conspicuous landmark of Williamson's Monument, a fine cairn erected in 1803 as a memorial to a local worthy and recently restored after partial collapse.

In an elevated field nearby are the extensive remains of an ancient British settlement, sited, as most were, well above the then swampy valleys, the early settlers living communally in hut villages. This one at Hugill is a good example; it is surrounded by an embankment intended more to define the village than to defend it, the area within forming an irregular pattern of streets. The drystone walls have not survived the weather of centuries but the foundations and footways between can still be discerned. The original boundary wall for most of its length has been used as the foundation of the present farm wall.

Other similar ancient sites found in the valley suggest that Kentmere was probably more populated in the years BC than it is AD.

Resuming the journey up the valley after crossing Scroggs Bridge, the road comes alongside a pleasant woodland carpeted by wild daffodils in springtime and continues between fragrant hedgerows flanked by trees that permit occasional glimpses of an exciting skyline ahead. A terrace of cottages is a reminder of lead mining activity in the area, and after a further pleasant two miles the buildings of an industrial complex appear on the left. These were established following the discovery of deposits of diatomaceous earth in the bed of the former lake which, when extracted and processed, provided a valuable insulation material. Supplies were sufficient to keep the works employed for many years; when exhausted, a proposal to conduct similar operations at Skeggles Water, a tarn a mile distant on the eastern ridge of the valley, failed to get planning permission and was abandoned. The bed of the lake yielded other surprises: two primitive boats, thought to be of Viking or Saxon age, were dug out of the mud, one being given to the National Maritime Museum and the other, incomplete, to Kendal Museum.

Amazingly, since operations ceased, a new Kent Mere has risen out of the ashes of the old lake, a sheet of water half a mile long having formed on the same site. The road, now clear of trees and with Kentmere church seen ahead across open fields, passes another terrace of cottages, behind which are the scanty remains of an ancient settlement. It then arrives at a fork, the right branch climbing to the farming community of Green Quarter and continuing to its terminus at Hollowbank (Hallow Bank on the current OS maps), the left going ahead to Low Bridge, where there was once an inn, and rising sharply to the church.

Kentmere church across the valley

Kentmere Hall

The origins of the parish church of St Cuthbert are obscure, the early records having been lost, but although much of the masonry and roof timbers are sixteenth-century it is thought there was a much earlier structure of the Saxon or Norman period. In 1806 a major restoration was undertaken. The church stands on an eminence in the middle of the valley and commands a splendid view.

A short lane turns left from the church and leads to the most interesting house in the valley, Kentmere Hall, which retains a fourteenth-century pele tower of four storeys with a vaulted cellar and a staircase, the manor house adjoining being of rather later date. It was originally the seat of the Gilpin family, a notable member of which was Bernard Gilpin, born here in 1577, who had a distinguished career in the Church and became known as the Apostle of the North. There is a memorial to him in St Cuthbert's. The Hall is now occupied as a farm.

From the church, where there is space for the parking of a few cars, the road goes on to a group of buildings on the left; here the track over Garburn Pass to Troutbeck starts. The road, now gated, continues to the last farm in the valley, Hartrigg, where it ends on the threshold of an exciting scene ahead. The towering cliffs of Rainsborrow Crag compel the attention as the most commanding feature of a high skyline around the head of the valley which effectively closes all exits. A rough quarry track goes forward from the end of the road, passing below first a high bank on which another ancient settlement has been discovered and then the scree slopes falling from the Crag, to enter a dead world of disused quarries and spoil heaps. Some relief from a depressing scene of devastation is afforded by the waters of Kentmere Reservoir although this too is disused and abandoned. Sad indeed is the industrial graveyard of upper Kentmere.

In the mid-nineteenth century, fifteen mills on the banks of the River Kent were drawing water from the river for driving their machinery. This was their only source of power and often in times of drought production was halted or restricted. To avert this occasional failure of supplies, an Act of Parliament in 1845 authorised the construction of reservoirs in the valleys of the Kent and its tributaries, the Mint and the Sprint, to be administered by Commissioners (the mill owners) for the purpose of impounding water that could be released when needed to maintain an adequate flow in the rivers. Five reservoirs were planned but only one was completed – Kentmere Head Reservoir, as it was then named, built in 1848. The others were not proceeded with because of excessive cost.

Walkers may persist along the side of the reservoir passing below the huge pyramid of Ill Bell, which may be climbed from here but only by unremitting effort, and continue into the final recess of Hall Cove, where a slender waterfall relieves an unfriendly landscape. High on the left, succeeding Ill Bell, is Froswick, a vast downfall of scree prohibiting direct ascent. The steep and pathless slope ahead, terminating the valley, may be climbed by an undignified scramble to Thornthwaite Crag or the plateau of High Street. If no such ascents are in mind, the return down the valley must be made by reversing the line of approach (unless a round walk, described below, is planned).

On the return journey, Rainsborrow Crag comes into view with even more dramatic effect, appearing as a shadowed silhouette against a bright sky. An adit at the base of the wall of rock indicates that the crag has been quarried internally and the fans of scree pouring from it confirm this. The gloomy industrial wasteland is succeeded by the pastures of Hartrigg and the road back to the village. Before reaching the church a short diversion along the Garburn path leads to Kentmere's biggest boulder, variously known as Badger Rock and Brock Stone; this may be seen in a field on the left past the buildings.

The higher reaches of the valley on the east side beyond Low Bridge offer an attractive walk, with some climbing, along an old packhorse route to the upper extremity of Kentmere at Nan Bield Pass. A side road turns off at Low Bridge to meet another at a difficult junction (for cars) near Green Quarter. It then rises steadily, gated, to the little colony of Hollowbank, passing an old track which leads over to Longsleddale. An insensitive highway authority proposed some years ago to overlay this with tarmac for the benefit of touring motorists but got no support for the plan.

Near the foot of the incline to the buildings of Hollowbank, a signposted footpath (to Mardale) branches left through attractive fields set above the river, and a short detour reveals the cascades of Kent Falls. Footpaths lead on to the reservoir so a round walk can be made if wished.

Badger Rock

The River Kent

On the higher level past Hollowbank, Overend Farm is next reached and the path continues thence up the valley below the steep slopes of Kentmere Pike to a tributary of the Kent, Ullstone Gill, which is crossed in a pretty dell.

Ahead now is the long climb to Nan Bield Pass. The path, waymarked by cairns and a fading milestone, rises across the flank of Tongue Scar at the base of which many generations of badgers have made their homes and have no wish to be disturbed. As height is gained, a large perched boulder, the Ull Stone, may be seen to the right near a disused quarry. A level mile follows, affording a splendid view of the Ill Bell range on the left, and finally a steep slope where progress is assisted by a series of excellent zigzags, leads to the top of Nan Bield Pass. This is crowned by a wind shelter of stones that offers a crumb of comfort in bad weather.

At 2100ft above the sea, Nan Bield is a perfect pass, steep on both sides with its crest forming a well-defined gap between high fells. It has a glorious view forward into Mardale; its brightest jewel, Small Water, is seen aerially, and the distant Pennines are in the background. It is my favourite mountain pass. And, looking back, the valley of Kentmere can be seen building up to this point. Nobody standing on Nan Bield Pass can doubt that Kentmere comes to a sudden end here.

45

THE TROUTBECK VALLEY

THERE ARE TWO Troutbecks within the National Park, one of them very familiar to residents in the Windermere area and to visitors who sojourn there, the other more remote from tourist centres and less well known. The subject of this chapter is the Windermere Troutbeck, a prize exhibit of Westmorland until Whitehall decreed in 1974 that the name of the county should be effaced from the map and replaced by Cumbria, a change not to the liking of most Westmorland folk. But a change in administration does not change the landscape, and Troutbeck under its new flag remains as lovely and as sweetly seductive as ever. Nor do traditions change. Troutbeck still appoints a Mayor without the authority of law and there is nothing Whitehall can do about that.

Troutbeck is the name of a valley and of the village within it, and Trout Beck is the stream that nurtures its emerald pastures. Three roads lead into the valley from the busy A591, the one most in use being the A592 which leaves the town of Windermere at a miniature roundabout, bound for Patterdale and Ullswater, to enter a pleasant suburbia of elegant residences and spacious gardens mostly created by Lancashire mill owners in Victorian times. Most notable of these is the estate of Holehird, generously bequeathed after the last war as a Cheshire Home for disabled servicemen; part of the extensive parklike grounds is occupied as gardens by the Lakeland Horticultural Society to which the public have free access and a welcome.

The Lakeland Horticultural Society's gardens at Holehird

Troutbeck church

Views of the valley ahead open as the road goes on to reach Troutbeck's parish church on the left, a neat structure with the unusual name of Jesus Church, formerly Jesus Chapel, since its consecration in 1562. The original building fell into a ruinous condition and was rebuilt in 1736. Major restorations and alterations followed in 1861, many of the earlier features being retained. A side lane to the left leaves here and rises to the village which straggles the fellside at a higher level. On the right, a rough lane leads upwards to Applethwaite Common, a venue for sheepdog trials, rising past a disused quarry to Garburn Pass and then descends into the Kentmere valley: this old track, unfit for cars, is still named Garburn Road on Ordnance Survey maps and was probably an important trade route in centuries past.

Beyond the church, the A592 passes a large caravan park that does nothing to enhance the scenery and indeed considerably detracts from it, and then rises to the north end of the village, Town Head, giving access along the way to two well-known hotels, the Mortal Man and the Queen's Head. The former is long distinguished by a signboard with the following couplet:

> Thou mortal man that lives by bread
> How comes thy nose to be so red?
> Thou silly ass that looks so pale
> It is by drinking Sally Birkett's ale.

The Queen's Head has traditional associations with the Mayor of Troutbeck.

At Town Head, the road is joined by the side lane from the village, after which the steep climb to Kirkstone Pass commences along the side of Wansfell with deepening views of the valley down on the right glimpsed through a fringe of trees. At the top of the sharp incline as the road curves west, a lovely bird's-eye prospect is seen on the right of Troutbeck Park Farm far below at the foot of The Tongue with the Ill Bell range an impressive background. The road then leaves the domain of Troutbeck and undulates at a high level to Kirkstone Pass. On the right is the minor upland valley of Woundale, which has no pedestrian paths and nothing deserving a separate heading. Its one merit is the direct approach it offers to Caudale Moor.

A more direct approach to the village leaves the A591 at Troutbeck Bridge, where Trout Beck enters upon the last stage of its journey before discharging into the waters of Windermere. It flows alongside the fields of Calgarth, the site of a large wartime establishment of temporary homes accommodating workers engaged in the construction of aeroplanes at a factory at nearby White Cross Bay; all traces of this occupation were removed after the war and replaced by Lakes School.

A side road from the bridge rises to a complex of buildings and is joined by another coming up from the A591 at Low Wood. Near the junction is a house of great character, notable for the outstanding excellence of its oak woodwork and unique furniture: this is Town End, dating from 1623 when it succeeded another house on the same site. It was built as the family home of the Brownes and occupied as such until 1947. It was then acquired by the National Trust and opened to the public.

The road goes on beyond Town End to enter the village, soon being bordered by a medley of fine residences and humble cottages in a variety of architectural styles. This adds pleasure and interest to its mile-long perambulation, a general air of activity creating the atmosphere of a busy street rather than a country road. The buildings are ranged along a high shelf on the sunny side of the valley and sheltered by the slopes of Wansfell behind. But Troutbeck is not always favoured and privileged by its beautiful environment. One wild day in June 1953, the placid life of its inhabitants was rudely shattered by a violent cloudburst on Wansfell that caused severe flooding and damage, an occurrence treated by the press almost as a national disaster. Even in Paradise there are times when black clouds obscure the blue sky.

The road through the village descends to join the A592 at Town Head. The naming of the extremities of the village as Town Head and Town End, and the appointment of a Mayor, seem to suggest that the earlier residents had an exalted sense of status and importance. Troutbeck is not a town. It is a village, an extremely pleasant village.

Town End

Town Head

Troutbeck Park Farm and The Tongue

Town Head is the key to the higher reaches of the valley, a lane leading to Troutbeck Park, a lovely area exclusively for travellers on foot. A side road, Ing Lane, turns off the A592 here, providing access to the remote Troutbeck Park Farm, and is soon joined by a footpath also leaving the A592 nearby. Classified as a bridleway and not intended for tourist traffic, the lane heads north in very pleasant surroundings, crossing Trout Beck at Ing Bridge. This is historic ground, being the way the Roman surveyors came nearly two thousand years ago when prospecting a route to link their forts at *Galava* (Ambleside) and *Brocavum* (Brougham). The result of their investigations was the loftiest road in the country, reaching an elevation of 2700ft on the fell, now known as High Street.

Around a corner beyond Ing Bridge, the farm is seen directly ahead, delightfully positioned on the lower slopes of a huge pyramid of high ground that effectively bars further progress forward and divides the valley into two side channels. This is The Tongue, one of many similar formations so named in the district although no other has the same colourful furnishings of trees and shrubs and heather, all donated by nature, as this one in Troutbeck Park.

The Tongue deflects walkers, as it did the Romans, to the watercourse of Hagg Gill descending along its eastern base. Here a good track bordered by a wall heads upstream in a cutting enclosed by The Tongue on the left and the massive Ill Bell range on the right. After a long straight mile, at a hiccup in the wall, the stream changes course, coming down the slopes of Froswick under the name of Blue Gill, and here too the Romans left the easy contours and started their long climb over the fells to *Brocavum*, their route being a groove slanting up to the skyline near Thornthwaite Crag, nowadays identified by a tall obelisk on the summit. This section of their road is known as Scots Rake following a skirmish here between native Britons and invading Scots during the times of the Border raids.

Troutbeck Valley from The Tongue

Instead of following in the steps of the Romans, an arduous exercise, the wall may be kept alongside as it continues north into a wild and pathless amphitheatre formed by the stony declivities of Caudale Moor and Thornthwaite Crag, linked at a breach in the skyline directly ahead. This gap is Threshthwaite Mouth, a watershed terminating the Troutbeck valley and the source of Trout Beck, which elects to descend along the west side of The Tongue. As the slopes of The Tongue decline, the wall also crosses to the west side and from it a detour may be made by an easy climb to the summit of The Tongue where at 1191ft a glorious view rewards the effort. The full length of the valley is displayed, with the lake of Windermere a lovely climax.

A return to the access road along the west base amongst trees and in the company of Trout Beck, which is crossed at one point by a seventeenth-century slate bridge, completes the circuit of The Tongue and the exploration of the Troutbeck valley.

THRESHTHWAITE GLEN

The Scottish influence on Lakeland place names is evident the nearer the approach to the Border: the word 'Glen' has been adopted for some of the valleys, either as a prefix (Glenridding) or following a location (Caiston Glen). But in no case do they match the verdant and impressive splendour of the Highland glens. Threshthwaite Glen, for instance, is a barren defile without beauty or charm, to which the usual 'dale' would be more appropriate and better suited. This is no place for picnic parties and searchers of natural grandeur. I have met only sheep.

The glen is hidden from the sight of car-bound tourists but can be entered, by strong walkers only, from Threshthwaite Mouth at the head of the Troutbeck valley, descending from this watershed to be guided down the glen by Pasture Beck: it is a long march with no hope of shelter or refreshment until it is ended.

The glen may be reached much more easily from the village of Hartsop, formerly Low Hartsop, which is reached along a short lane from a crossroads on the A592 near Brothers Water. Hartsop is a delightful old settlement rooted in mediaeval times, a throwback to Lakeland as it was before Victorian sightseers discovered it. It still retains primitive buildings and an upper spinning gallery. A few modern bungalows have sprouted on the fellside but Hartsop prefers to remain an outdoor museum of seventeenth-century Lakeland. A new car park at the top of the lane is an anachronism in a place where for ages past horses and carts have been the only forms of transport. Hartsop Dodd, the conical height towering behind the buildings and self-appointed guardian of the village, sheds tears as it looks down on this insensitive innovation and is not the only one to do so. Hartsop and the twentieth century are strangers to each other and not even on speaking terms. Hartsop is precious.

Hartsop Dodd

One merit of the car park is the view it has opened of the wild hinterland of Hartsop, a surround of rough fells dominated by Gray Crag directly ahead with a stream tumbling down its north side from the hidden reservoir of Hayeswater behind to join Pasture Beck. The path to Threshthwaite Glen crosses Walker Bridge alongside and skirts an area of devastation where the levels and shafts of abandoned lead-mine workings may be traced and turns a corner into the glen with Pasture Beck in close company. The beck provides the only life and movement in a sterile defile between stony and desolate fellsides, whilst the buttress of Raven Crag falling from the high skyline on the right is the only feature to arrest attention. Then the lonely hollow of Threshthwaite Cove is reached at the foot of grassy slopes watered by streams that unite effectively to form Pasture Beck. The slope may be climbed to Threshthwaite Mouth, the watershed ending the glen and linking Thornthwaite Crag and Caudale Moor, but unless the ascent of one of these is intended there is little point in proceeding beyond the Cove, the only reward being a fine prospect of the Troutbeck valley from the divide. Poor Threshthwaite Glen; it has so little to offer.

View to Threshwaite Glen from Brothers Water

52

Pasture Beck   *Stock Ghyll Force*

Stock Gill

ARCADIA COME TRUE is the Stock Ghyll Force, a waterfall plunging sixty feet in twin channels down a rocky dell in a bower of lovely trees. This is a delightful picture of sylvan beauty and charm, the finest of its kind in Lakeland and is also Ambleside's number one scenic attraction. Above the Force, however, all is anticlimax, the stream coming down a shallow valley with no other highlights. Here it retains the original spelling of Stock Gill, the word 'ghyll' being a romantic adaptation of the name by the early Victorian visitors to the waterfall.

The road to Stock Ghyll Force leaves Ambleside behind the Salutation Hotel and from it a path branches left into a pleasant park. In my much younger days, a charge for admission was made and never resented, so great was the privilege conferred. The path is directed by the sound of rushing water to the top of the falls and a lower viewing platform where a delightful picture of sylvan beauty and charm, enhanced by the falling water, is perfectly posed for the camera.

The Kirkstone Pass from Stock Gill

The road may be rejoined from the top of the falls and continued left, becoming an access to Middle Grove Farm; this is the only remaining habitation in the upper valley, Low Grove and High Grove having vanished. Once clear of the trees, Kirkstone Pass is seen directly ahead with Red Screes forming a massive whaleback to the left: the slopes rising immediately on the right lead to the top of Wansfell. Beyond Middle Grove, a worsening track goes forward to the site of High Grove, and it is difficult to appreciate that this was the usual route to Kirkstone Pass before the present motor road was made at a higher level on the west side of the valley. The former road climbed the grassy slope from High Grove to join the road coming from Windermere, now the A592, but this final section has now gone to seed and a path crosses to the road from Ambleside at Pett's Bridge, under which flows Stock Gill on its way down from Red Screes.

At Pett's Bridge, the road starts a daunting incline to Kirkstone Pass Inn, known as The Struggle in the days of horsedrawn traffic and as the valley of Stock Gill ends here, a quick return may be made to Ambleside along the road. If, however, the prospect of a drink at the inn impels the feet up the hill, a secondary objective could be the location of the source of Stock Gill on the grassy expanse beyond the car park opposite the inn.

PATTERDALE

MOST VISITORS TO Lakeland relate the name of Patterdale to the small village so-called near the head of Ullswater, rarely to the delightful valley of which the village is the 'tourist' capital and which gets my vote as the most attractive. This is an opinion reinforced in recent years as its main contenders, Borrowdale and Langdale, whilst losing nothing of their beauty and grandeur, have become untenable by seekers after undisturbed peace because of the increasing weight of holiday traffic, the influx of cars and coaches and caravans bringing crowds of sightseers and the inevitable consequences of commercial developments to cater for them. Patterdale too has daily visitations of cars and coaches but in lesser numbers, and here it is still possible, especially in early morning and late evening, to sense again the absolute quiet and tranquillity of Lakeland a century ago. In Patterdale you can still hear the singing of birds and the murmur of streams above the sound of vehicles.

The valley, set deep amongst fells of individual distinction but alike in their invitation, is remarkable for its rapid transition from primeval wildness to pastoral greenery and native woodlands, and for its beautiful lake of serpentine curves, which also gets my vote as the fairest of all.

Patterdale is also unusual in its many offshoots, smaller side valleys of no less charm, all eager to contribute their waters to the main valley stream, all with a welcome and anxious to please. Patterdale is parent to many infant dales and sets a pattern of loveliness his family try to emulate.

The Patterdale valley starts to take shape from Kirkstone Pass, a narrow defile descending sharply between the rocky slope of Red Screes and the long scree runs of Caudale Moor in a surround of desolation, tamed only by the slender ribbon of tarmac of the A592 which does nothing to relieve the grim bleakness of the scene but merely emphasises it. Amongst the tumble of boulders fallen from Red Screes is the one that gave the Pass its name, the Kirk Stone. Perched only a few yards to the left of the road near a new car park, this landmark is conspicuous on the long climb from the north, its silhouette on the skyline resembling a ridged church tower.

Adding a sparkle of life to a dead scene, Kirkstone Beck has its origins near the Kirkstone Pass Inn and leaps in cascades alongside the road as though eager to escape from its wild setting to reach the pleasant pastures seen still distant in the valley ahead and far below. The view north from the Pass is arresting. Several miles of the valley can be seen aerially, the transformation in colour from black to green being striking. Brothers Water appears as a jewel in the middle distance and Place Fell forms the background with a glint of Ullswater to its left.

The Kirk Stone

55

Patterdale from the Kirkstone Pass

The Kirkstone road is unkind to pedestrians, tight enclosing walls preventing escape to the verges from speeding traffic, but on the descent north a signpost on the left offers a pleasant alternative. A path following Kirkstone Beck downstream curves around the base of Middle Dodd, leaving austerity behind as trees and green fields appear ahead. A side valley opens on the left, bringing down a tributary, Caiston Beck. This side valley is Caiston Glen.

CAISTON GLEN

Caiston Glen is a short straight trench coming down from Scandale Pass. Carrying a path from Ambleside that bypasses Kirkstone Pass entirely, it has therefore, for the walker, much to commend it although it is lacking in interest. Caiston Glen descends between Middle Dodd and High Hartsop Dodd, both falling in steep and rough slopes to the beck. High Hartsop Dodd, normally unassuming and unfrequented, had a brief period of fame for several days in 1948; older readers will remember the national press coverage given to the efforts of the dalesmen to rescue two terriers trapped in a cavity in the rocks below the summit during a fox hunt, a mission of mercy rewarded with success but only after more than a week's sustained digging and removal of boulders; the outcome was a cause for rejoicing.

The path goes forward, in surroundings becoming more sylvan, to Hartsop Hall at a walkers' crossroads; this is a farmhouse of distinction, indeed, the Hall was built over a right of way and in the early years walkers had the privilege of walking through the house from one door to another until the path was diverted around the buildings. From here there is access to the A592 at the Brothers-water Hotel.

I never pass the Brotherswater Hotel without remembering the biggest meal I ever had. Lakeland's innkeepers and boarding-house landladies are renowned for their generous helpings of food and well-laden tables, but all were excelled and records broken one teatime when I called after a day on the fells. I was welcomed to an empty dining-room. I was not surprised to be alone there: the time was just after the war and rationing was still in force. But I was not prepared for what was to follow. After a brief wait, three huge platefuls were placed before me, one after another, which I duly despatched. I was then ready to go but the innkeeper told me to stay and in the next half-hour produced a fourth course and a fifth and a sixth and a seventh despite my cries of 'Enough!' It gradually occurred to me that the man had catered for a party of ramblers who had failed to arrive. I was both a benefactor and a sufferer of their default: when I was finally allowed to leave on payment of five shillings, I found the heavy meal had put a severe brake on my movements as I toiled over Kirkstone Pass and down to the last bus from Ambleside.

DOVEDALE

Hartsop Hall stands at the entrance to one of the most beautiful short valleys in Lakeland. A path rises steeply alongside a wall and a coppice wood where it was once possible, and probably still is, to fill the rucksack with hazel nuts at the right time of year, although I found the difficulty of breaking open the shells never justified the trouble of collection. The upper recesses of Dovedale, a tortured landscape of hillocks and hollows below the imposing buttress of Dove Crag, now a network of serious rock-climbing routes and out of bounds to ordinary mortals, is a fascinating area to explore. Hunsett Cove and The Stangs especially reveal much of interest on close inspection. Dove Falls are formed by a stream issuing from the Cove and can be seen from the path. This watercourse later joins Hogget Gill coming down a ravine on the south side of The Stangs, their combined waters, after a brief journey together, discharging into Kirkstone Beck near the Hall.

Dovedale is only a mile in length, but it is a mile of pleasure.

Dovedale

Brothers Water

THE WALK DOWN the main valley continues north beyond Hartsop Hall on an access lane bordered by Low Wood, and comes alongside Brothers Water. This is a placid and pleasant lake of small extent but not as innocent as appearances suggest, having on its conscience the death by drowning of two brothers on separate occasions during the early years of the last century. This double tragedy led to a change in the name of the lake, hitherto known as Broad Water. The issuing stream is Goldrill Beck, as pretty as its name, and here the lane ends at a junction with the A592.

From the junction, travellers on foot can avoid the A592 and its traffic by taking instead a quiet byroad from the nearby Hartsop crossroads that leads in two miles to Patterdale village.

DEEPDALE

The A592 next arrives at Deepdale Bridge, here crossing a large stream that indicates the presence of another side valley, unseen behind a screen of trees but soon revealed on the left with a minor road leading into it. This is Deepdale.

Deepdale has much in common with neighbouring Dovedale, both draining the Fairfield fells on parallel courses only a mile apart, but they are not twins. Deepdale is much longer and has a flat strath of cultivated pastures and a few habitations, all lacking in Dovedale, nor is it initially as beautiful and exciting. But beyond the last farm, Wallend, an easy path goes forward in the close company of Deepdale Beck and rounds the base of St Sunday Crag and now the landscape suddenly erupts in a savage display of rocky skylines. Hart Crag is directly ahead but more compelling is the nearer towering pyramid of Greenhow End, and this is succeeded by a series of buttresses and scree runs forming the north flank of Fairfield. Around the corner of St Sunday Crag, the path rises less distinctly to the end of the valley at Deepdale Hause.

Beyond the entrance to Deepdale, the main road skirts the base of Arnison Crag and passes a modern Youth Hostel, purpose built and more palatial than most. Then, around the bend, Patterdale village is immediately ahead, looking exactly as I first saw it sixty years ago except for a car park and more springtime daffodils. I like places that do not change, that remain content to be as they have always been. Familiarity is supposed to bring contempt; here, for me, it brings only a feeling of nostalgia, a revival of happy memories of days long gone.

Village is perhaps too grand a word for this little settlement of two hotels, a post office and a few cottages in a sweet simplicity of arrangement. I have a soft spot for the post office, this being the first shop to offer to sell copies of my first guidebook to the fells: an order for six was repeated within a week, a cause of much inward rejoicing and relief since I had incurred a debt of £900 with a local printer. Some of the cottages I remember with affection, being always welcomed for overnight or longer stays and being treated with kindness and solicitude – especially on wet days when I came in soaked. Then great concern was shown for my comfort and well-being. One day in particular I remember well, when an unceasing deluge of rain from dawn to dusk kept me penned indoors, the kind lady of the house beseeching me not to venture outside: never was a prisoner treated with more consideration for his welfare.

Patterdale is a nice place to be, in any weather.

Upper Deepdale

Patterdale village   Below *Patterdale church*

Patterdale village is a centre of excellence for excursions on foot in a lovely countryside liberally endowed by nature and not significantly disturbed by the works and influences of that greatest of spoilers, man. There are splendid mountains to climb, including the mighty Helvellyn, a wide choice of fells to wander over and explore, valley rambles of exquisite charm and, putting the seal on perfection, paths along the shores of the most beautiful of the lakes, Ullswater.

Patterdale seems too good for this poor polluted earth. When I try to visualise heaven, it is not St Peter at the gate and angels sitting on clouds that I see but a paradise modelled on Patterdale with happy hikers on the fells and the Abraham Brothers as gatekeepers.

At the north end of the village, around a corner, is St Patrick's Church, erected in 1853 and given parochial status in 1866. Since my early visits, the tower has been furnished with a useful but oddly placed clock.

Grisedale

GRISEDALE

Wild boars must have been rampant in Lakeland in bygone times, five valleys still preserving their old name of grise, and of these the best known today is the one breaching the barrier of the Fairfield—Helvellyn range which carries a pedestrian route over the watershed to Grasmere and a main feeder of Ullswater through scenery of the highest order.

The road into Grisedale leaves the A592 near Patterdale church, rising steadily to the left and ending after a mile. Here a congestion of unattended cars indicates the starting point for a popular ascent of Helvellyn by way of Striding Edge, the path thereto initially going down a field and crossing Grisedale Beck. The tarmac road is succeeded by a cart track heading up the valley towards a skyline that looks more impressive and daunting with every step, contrasting starkly with the lush meadows and pastures of the approach. High on the left of the track, the slopes of Birks merge into the towering pyramid of St Sunday Crag, identified by a line of cliffs below the summit; ahead and to the right Dollywaggon Pike and Nethermost Pike, outliers of Helvellyn, soar into the sky above uninviting downfalls of crags and scree.

Beyond the last farm, Elmhow and a small plantation, Grisedale Beck is crossed. Here the easy walking ends and a rough path climbs towards Dollywaggon's most intimidating aspect: the shadowed cliffs of Falcon Crag rising out of the dark recesses of Cock Cove. Seen to the right during the ascent is another of Lakeland's many Eagle Crags, this one a resort of rock-climbers. The gradient eases as the lonely building of Ruthwaite Lodge is reached alongside a waterfall with a disused mine lever at the foot: this former shooting hut is now occupied by a climbing club. A gentle incline continues to the outlet of Grisedale Tarn, and nearby, in a tumble of rocks, is an inscribed boulder known as the Brothers' Parting which is where Wordsworth said a last farewell to his brother John in 1805. They never met again, John being drowned shortly afterwards in the ship he commanded. The tarn, a large expanse of water that invariably brings footsteps to a halt, is rounded by the old pony route from Grasmere to Helvellyn and this well-worn track may be followed up a simple rise to the end of the valley at the watershed of Grisedale Hause at 1929ft.

The wild boars and the eagles have gone from Grisedale but their long absence has not robbed the valley of excitement and interest. It is a place where every visit, no matter how often repeated, is as fresh as the first.

Glenridding

BEYOND PATTERDALE CHURCH and the turn into Grisedale, the A592 enters the village of Glenridding, passing on the way the ornate St Patrick's Well on the roadside. From here is the first glimpse of Ullswater. The busy main street has shops in variety, car parks, guest houses and hotels and, in the holiday season, crowds of visitors.

The emancipation of Glenridding from a humble mining community to a popular holiday resort has been rapid, especially since the closing of the large Greenside Lead Mine, on which the economy of the village once depended. Tourism is the new bread-winner. It is true that the early Victorian sightseers, arriving in horse-drawn carriages, discovered the place and, attracted by the proximity of Ullswater, sojourned here and were catered for, but it was the post-war boom in car and coach travel, still increasing, that has transformed its fortunes.

THE VALLEY OF GLENRIDDING BECK

A side road turns off alongside the descending Glenridding Beck to the upper part of the village where the miners had their homes, and can be continued to the site of the mine; this is now grassed over, its buildings dismantled or converted. Some evidence of the former industry may be traced by continuing forward up the valley in the close company of the beck. This leads below the towering peak of Catstycam to the breached dam of Keppelcove Tarn, once a reservoir for the mine but now dry. Other paths climb from the upper valley to the Helvellyn range, and Redtarn Beck, coming down the side of Catstycam, points the way to a direct ascent of Helvellyn itself. Another path zigzags up the fellside on the right just beyond the mine and crosses an underground flue to the site of a former chimney on the side of Raise.

62

The pier at Glenridding   Below *Glencoyne Farm with its cylindrical chimney stacks*

LEAVING GLENRIDDING ON its journey north, the A592 soon reaches a delightful section along the shore of Ullswater, where Wordsworth saw ten thousand daffodils at a glance and was inspired by the sight to write his best-known poem, and not even the threatening roadside cliff of Stybarrow Crag can dispel the charm of the scenery hereabouts. Further on, a track on the left leads through trees to a hidden row of cottages well-named Seldom Seen, and then the entrance to the side valley of Glencoyne is reached on the left.

GLENCOYNE

Glencoyne's principal feature of interest is the solitary habitation of Glencoyne farmhouse, the cylindrical chimney stacks being an architectural joy. A path rises through the valley along the side of Sheffield Pike and above the descending Glencoyne Beck, to reach Sticks Pass.

An area of the indefinite high ground bordering the valley on the north was recently renamed Birkett Fell and a memorial cairn built to immortalise Lord Birkett, a true friend of Lakeland, whose efforts to preserve the sanctity and beauty of Ullswater thwarted plans to convert the lake into a reservoir.

64

THE VALLEY OF AIRA BECK

NOT ALL STREAMS flow in well-defined valleys; some meander through fields and others find their way along minor channels, and although Aira Beck, seen on a map, follows a long and tortuous course, only its formative tributaries, coming down from Great Dodd, have the characteristics of deep and enclosed cuttings. These origins are in wild and inhospitable territory more akin to the Pennines than Lakeland, unfrequented, not tourist country at all, without paths other than those made by sheep for the exclusive use of sheep, with tracts of marshy ground that impede progress on foot.

An access road leaves High Row, a mile from Dockray, and ends at the lonely outpost of Dowthwaitehead where even some fine trees fail to relieve an atmosphere of sadness, dereliction and neglect following an exodus of population. It is not an area of cherished memories, but I recall a sighting I had never seen before nor have I since: a gathering of buzzards, about twenty in number, feeding on the ground on a patch of grass half the size of a tennis court. These, and sheep, were the only creatures I saw on that day's walk. I make no recommendation for the exploration of the upper reaches of Aira Beck and its environs. Visitors here will wish they had gone elsewhere.

But, in maturity, the beck develops an alluring beauty, the later stages presenting a scene so magnetic that visitors are drawn to it in crowds.

Leaving Glencoyne, the A592 persists along the lovely shores of Ullswater to a junction with a road to Dockray and Keswick on the left, and alongside is a group of buildings and a car park catering for the daily invasion of tourists to see Aira Force. From here a charming path leads in a few minutes to a rustic bridge where there suddenly appears a picture so spectacular and of such bewitching charm that

viewers are stopped in their tracks and remain rooted. The beck is seen emerging from an upper bridge at the top of a rocky ravine, down which, excited by a first glimpse of Ullswater waiting for it far below, it leaps in ecstasy, eager to reach its lakeside rendezvous. This waterfall is Aira Force, a perfect subject for the camera, and may in fact be reached with less effort from a car park on the Dockray road. A path goes forward to the higher bridge and continues upstream to a more modest waterfall, High Force. Beyond is anticlimax and there is little point in proceeding further unless a visit to the small village of Dockray is needed to replenish the stomach or the rucksack.

Left *Aira Force*
Right *High Force, Aira Beck*

MATTERDALE

NORTH-EAST OF DOCKRAY is an extensive agricultural area which, although within the National Park, is rarely mentioned in guidebooks and seldom included in the itineraries of tourists. Apart from the two minor heights of Great and Little Mell Fell, there is nothing to attract fellwalkers in a district more suited to simple rambles along a network of country lanes; there is little chance of refreshment and hospitality from a scattered community whose business is farming not tourism. The scenery is pleasant, with some charming corners, but unexciting, in character more akin to a rural shire than to Lakeland. With the charms of Ullswater beckoning only a few miles away and the manifold attractions of Keswick a mere half-hour's drive, there are few visitors: a stranger met wandering here may safely be assumed to have lost his way, or his map.

It is an area of undulations, streams flowing through shallow depressions to enter Ullswater directly, or preferring to drain into Aira Beck and reach the lake by a more circuitous and thrilling journey. Of these watercourses, only one is in what aspires to be called a valley. This is Matterdale, also the name of the parish, its handsome church framed in trees alongside the A5091 north of Dockray. The church was built in the sixteenth century with a thatched roof, later alterations providing the present tower with stepped gables. One of the two fonts is thought to be Norman and an inscription cut in a beam carries the date 1573. The altar and communion rails are seventeenth-century. Nearby are the few buildings of Matterdale End, and a road along the valley branches here.

Matterdale church

The pier at Pooley Bridge

From the Dockray junction, the A592 closely follows the lakeside, giving a glimpse of the battlemented former shooting lodge of Lyulph's Tower on the left. The road arrives at the hamlet of Watermillock after skirting the base of Gowbarrow Fell. It here turns inland thus providing a wider lakeside strip of which a few fine houses and hotels have taken advantage, before returning to the shore for the last mile to Pooley Bridge at the foot of Ullswater, passing the landing pier of the passenger boats before entering the village. Here, in a holiday atmosphere, are shops, hotels and other accommodation, car parks, camp sites and moorings for small craft.

It was at Pooley Bridge that I first experienced an overnight stay at an hotel. Although in my mid-twenties, I had never previously even been inside an hotel: such establishments had always seemed too posh for a scruffy Lancashire lad like me. But on this occasion I was desperate for rest and refreshment, having had a long hard day on the High Street range and darkness had fallen when I entered the village. The place was quiet, out of season, and I was drawn like a moth to the only light I could see, which proved to be outside the door of an hotel, illuminating a sign that promised meals and bed and breakfast. I entered in a state of apprehension and asked the man behind the bar if I could have a meal and a bed for the night. He eyed me up and down and asked where I was from and, when I told him, he was instantly more friendly: he too was from Lancashire, Bolton. Yes, he would supply my needs, and after an excellent supper we fell to arguing the relative merits of Blackburn Rovers and Bolton Wanderers, there being no other visitors or callers that night. At ten o'clock we declared the match a draw and I retired to my appointed room. I rather enjoyed my first stay in an hotel.

Apart from the attractions of the lake, there are short walks in the vicinity of interest to antiquarians. The wooded hill of Dunmallet alongside has on its summit the sparse remains of a fort thought to date from Celtic times, and the nearby Moor Divock crossed by a Roman road is a treasure ground of ancient relics.

THE VALLEY OF THE RIVER EAMONT

SURPLUS WATER IN Ullswater is unobtrusively tunnelled and piped to supplement supplies in Haweswater by pumping and gravity, the natural outflow being taken by the River Eamont from the foot of the lake at Pooley Bridge and fed into the River Eden on its way to the Solway Firth. Although robbed of its full potential and denied its original right to drain Ullswater exclusively, the Eamont remains a considerable river as it enters and passes through a gentler landscape and widening contours and, after a few uneventful miles, departs from the National Park without ceremony. Joined by the River Lowther, it then heads for the greater valley of the Eden.

THE VALLEYS EAST OF ULLSWATER

TO THE EAST of Ullswater is a complex of valleys forming part of the lake's gathering grounds, yet so deeply enclosed by fells, so hidden from the sight of summer throngs of visitors on the pleasure boats and travellers on the A592, that they remain unsuspected. Moreover, there is no obvious road access and none of the valleys has a through route for motorists, and therefore the area is free from traffic disturbance and spared cheap commercial distractions. Here the sounds are of nature, not transistor radios; here life is lived as it should be lived. Here is the Lakeland of centuries ago.

BOARDALE

Boardale, alternatively spelt Boredale and Bore Dale in some guidebooks and maps, is introduced on a splendid circular walk, best done anti-clockwise. From the head of Ullswater, a rising path with glorious views of the Patterdale valley climbs to Boardale Hause, where there are a few remains of an ancient chapel. The path descends immediately to Boardalehead between Place Fell and Beda Fell, and then becomes a lane as solitary farm buildings are passed. At a junction it turns left to the few cottages of Sandwick, where the lakeside is rejoined and followed back to base on the most beautiful lakeside path in Lakeland, every step a delight, thus completing the circuit of Place Fell. Boardale itself is unexciting but heaven is glimpsed on the approach and exit.

FUSEDALE

A quiet road leaves Pooley Bridge and proceeds for five miles along the east side of Ullswater to arrive at the hotel and few houses of Howtown. The pier here is a regular calling place of the passenger boats, thereby offering an effortless alternative approach for visitors without cars. Behind the hotel and screened by trees is the long straight cutting of Fusedale, bringing down a stream from Wether Hill on the High Street range.

Martindale from Hallin Fell

I was in Fusedale only once, as a raw novice in fellwalking, and here was taught a lesson I needed to learn: never to wear smooth-soled footwear when walking on the hills. I had come along the easy and fairly level ridge from High Street and had passed over Wether Hill when the valley of Fusedale came into view far below on the left at the foot of an unbroken grass slope. I decided to call it a day and go down to search for a bed. I started to descend this inviting expanse of greenery, to find at once that my smooth-soled shoes could get no purchase on the short grass and after a few slips and tumbles found I could only proceed safely by shuffling down on my backside, using it as a brake. This I did through a thousand feet of height, mercifully without witnesses, before I could again stand upright.

MARTINDALE

From Howtown the road continues, spiralling up a steep fellside to disclose a beautiful view forward of the full length of Martindale. At first sight, one falls in love with Martindale. At the top of the incline from Howtown is the parish church of St Peter, built in 1882 to replace the old church of St Martin half a mile away. For many years, St Martin stood in ruins but it has been restored sufficiently to allow occasional services to be held.

The road continues up the valley along the base of Beda Fell, and approaches the long-established Martindale Deer Forest where the deer are unconfined and free to roam. The Nab, a deer reserve, here divides the valley into two branches, Bannerdale and Rampsgill; both branches bring down streams into the main valley where they unite under the name of Howgrain Beck and enter Ullswater at Sandwick. Martindale may also be reached by walkers along a path that leaves Boardale Hause and, guided by a wall, descends through Bannerdale.

PART TWO

The Southern Valleys

Seat Sandal from Grasmere
Left Vale of Grasmere from Loughrigg Terrace

The Lyth Valley from Scout Scar

THE LYTH VALLEY

THE ESTUARY OF the River Kent and the northern shore of Morecambe Bay receive many streams flowing south from the central heights of Lakeland. Some of these are minor watercourses in shallow channels that barely influence the landscape, others are halted and delayed in their progress by lakes and tarns they have formed, and yet others have carved deep passages through the fells. These streams vary greatly in length and characteristics, being alike only in direction, south to the open sea. The valleys that carry them there, nurtured by their waters down the ages, provide not only shelter but lovely environs.

West of the lower valley of the River Kent, and separated from it by the limestone escarpment of Underbarrow Scar, better known locally as Scout Scar, is the Lyth valley. This is an alluvial plain that appears to have once been an inlet of the estuary, long abandoned by the tidal waters that formed it: so flat is the surface of this plain that six miles inland from the coast the height of the ground is only a few feet above sea level. The valley, a mile wide, lies between the abrupt slopes of Scout Scar in the east and Whitbarrow in the west and at the head are small undulations carrying streams that combine to form the River Gilpin which then, without contours to speed its progress, proceeds sluggishly down the valley to pass under the A590 at Sampool Bridge and meander across an area of coastal mosses before discharging its waters into the River Kent. A fast road, the A5074, leaves the bridge and travels along the west side of the valley to Bowness-on-Windermere: a quieter and more attractive road prefers the east side and visits the charming villages of Levens and Brigsteer.

The village of Levens is reached from the A590 near Levens Bridge on the A6 and is a delightful medley of old cottages and modern bungalows blended together in a favoured position on high ground overlooking the valley and with an open aspect to the west. It is a sun trap for retired pensioners who seek to spend their later years in undisturbed peace and prefer to look at sunsets with little further concern for the affairs of the world outside. Levens gives the impression of a pleasant garden suburb set around the steepled church of St John the Evangelist, built in 1828 and preserving under cover in the churchyard its three original bells minus their clappers.

The road north from the village passes through the extensive Brigsteer Wood where mature native trees provide shelter for a springtime carpet of wild daffodils. Out of the wood, the road enters Brigsteer, a village quite unlike Levens. Brigsteer is older and looks its age. Brigsteer has wrinkles. Visitors whose lives are dictated by tidiness and orderly arrangements will be dismayed on seeing Brigsteer. There are few straight lines in this jumble of cottages and barns and workshops. Brigsteer belongs to a time before planning permissions were needed. The buildings are set at all angles, some fronting the road, others turning their backs and sides to it; the stone walls, where not crumbling, are mossy and lichened; flowers grow where not expected. Brigsteer is haphazard and not at all fussy; it just happened, bit by bit. In short, Brigsteer is entirely charming.

A steep road leaves here for Kendal, with access to Scout Scar, and another goes on to the equally pleasing village of Underbarrow. The supreme joy of the Lyth valley is its annual springtime renewal. Most of the farmsteads have a surround of damson trees which, in addition to providing a later delicious harvest, makes a glorious display of blossom when winter withdraws its forces, appearing as puffs of white smoke all over the valley.

The Lyth valley is outside the boundary of the National Park but, if the criterion for inclusion is beauty of scenery, richly qualifies.

Near Brigsteer Wood

THE WINSTER VALLEY

I HAVE NEVER been overfond of poetry nor troubled to memorise any, but two short verses seen in boyhood days have remained in my memory and can be recalled to mind without hesitation. One is Wordsworth's 'Daffodils' and the other, writer and title unknown, goes like this:

> When I went down to Winster, full fifty years ago,
> The vale was filled with blossom, wild cherry and the sloe.
> But the grace of all its graces
> And the charm of all its charms
> Was the snowy damson blossoms around the fellside farms.

These lines are perhaps even more appropriate to the neighbouring Lyth valley, which is more open and reveals its treasures at a glance. The Winster valley is more shy, with hidden corners, and much is concealed by rich woodlands and minor undulations: there are few distant vistas. The River Winster, baptised by that name from its place of birth amongst lovely foothills near Windermere Golf Course, has been deprived of its former proud function as the county boundary between Lancashire and Westmorland now that it is wholly in Cumbria, a change that left the stream undisturbed and unperturbed: the Winster flows today where the Winster has always flowed.

After passing under the A5074 it comes within sight of the inn and the few buildings of Winster and then heads south into the welcoming arms of mature trees in a native woodland. It comes alongside a byroad that passes the little church of the Holy Trinity and leads to a ford and footbridge in a shady hollow, an idyllic spot unless the river is in furious spate. Bowland Bridge is the next port of call and indeed the last, as the river, now more assured of its destination, flows through a widening valley in sylvan surroundings to skirt the scattered village of Witherslack. It passes under the A590 to empty into Morecambe Bay, after a journey of unblemished delight along a valley where all is fair to look upon. The Winster valley, like the Lyth, has good reason to be aggrieved at its exclusion from the National Park.

THE CARTMEL VALLEY

FEW OF THE many visitors to the village of Cartmel go there to see the valley it occupies or the stream that filters through it, both being quite insignificant as geographical features. Indeed, the valley is so shallow and indefinite that awareness of it is indicated only by the presence of the stream. This enters from the north after crossing the sweet pastures of Field Broughton under the name of Ayside Pool and departs to fulfil its destiny in Morecambe Bay.

The main attractions of a visit to Cartmel are, first and foremost, the magnificent Priory, the most notable monastic church in the north-west: the village, too, a place of quaint nooks and corners, is a delightful oyster for antiquarian explorers, and Cartmel Races bring an occasional flurry of visitors whose prime interests are centred neither on the Priory nor the village but on the nearby racecourse.

The Priory Church of St Mary and St Michael is an architectural gem that looks far too grand for the humble rural environs, even out of place: such elegance of design, such solidity and strength, would be more expected gracing the boulevards of a capital city.

The village of Cartmel and, below, *the Priory Church*

It was founded as a Priory of Canons Regular of St Augustine in the year 1188 by William Marshall, Baron of Cartmel, who later became the second Earl of Pembroke, and he endowed it with the manor and adjacent lands. He further ordained that the Priory should be free from subjection to any other religious house and that an altar should be provided with a priest for the people. By virtue of this latter condition, the monastery was preserved from destruction in the Dissolution of the sixteenth century.

Alterations to the fabric have proceeded down the years, and the interior, with its splendid east window, has become a treasury of sculptures and mediaeval glass, artifacts and timbers. One feels better, and more attuned to the circumstances of everyday life, after a visit to Cartmel Priory.

THE ROTHAY VALLEY

MOST VISITORS ENTER the Lake District at Windermere, arriving there along the much-improved A591 or by train, the final stage of their approach catching glimpses of a silver expanse of water receding for many miles to its southern extremities amongst wooded foothills where it appears almost like a wide river. This is Windermere the lake, a permanent guest of the Rothay valley, snugly occupying its floor for ten beautiful miles.

The Rothay valley is the most populated and busiest part of the district, having the towns of Windermere and Ambleside and the village of Grasmere within a short distance. It has the greatest concentration of holiday visitors, the influx increasing each year to such an extent that the amenities are subjected to severe pressure. Those like myself who remember the Rothay valley in pre-war days and went there to enjoy the undisturbed tranquillity and glorious scenery cannot fail to be concerned at the changes that have taken place and which are gathering momentum.

But crowds and traffic jams apart, let me affirm with emphasis that the scenery of the Rothay valley is one of unsurpassed beauty, a blending of natural features in perfect harmony, a landscape richly endowed with visual treasures, a symphony without a discordant note.

The Rothay valley starts to take shape on Dunmail Raise, a major watershed between north and south which is crossed by the main artery of communication, the A591. Recent improvements have converted the road into a fast highway from which heavy lorries are prohibited, and over the top of the pass a dual carriageway has been created to preserve undisturbed a huge pile of stones. This massive cairn reputedly marks the grave of Dunmail, the last King of Cumberland, who was defeated in battle in 945 by King Edmund of England.

Raise Beck comes down the side of Seat Sandal and, after surrendering some of its water by a diversion to Thirlmere, passes under the road on its original bed and heads south across an area of glacial drumlins alongside the road, which soon reveals a lovely view of Grasmere ahead. At a road junction on the right is a bungalow still named Toll Bar Cottage, indicating its purpose when the road was a narrow turnpike. The side road here goes down to the sequestered hamlet of Gill Foot, where Raise Beck is joined by a stream issuing from the Greenburn Valley and becomes the River Rothay.

The British National Sheepdog Trials, Grasmere

THE GREENBURN VALLEY

A track leaves Gill Foot, passing isolated cottages to enter the Greenburn valley, a defile largely hidden by the enclosing heights of Steel Fell and the Helm Crag—Calf Crag ridge. It is unfrequented, although the name of its stream, Green Burn, suggests that the Scots have been here. There is a pretty waterfall as the track continues to a sheepfold where the stream can be crossed to an indistinct droveway leading up to Calf Crag. The upper valley is marshy. The one merit of the Greenburn valley is the escape it provides from the noise and bustle of Grasmere.

A QUIET ROAD leaves Gill Foot for Grasmere, passing below the steep slopes of Helm Crag, better known to travellers on the A591 as the Lion and the Lamb because of a fancied resemblance in the summit rocks, and recognised with squeals of delight by passengers on the many coaches that daily tour the district. Short of the village, the road from Gill Foot joins another, this on most summer days carrying a procession of walkers bound for Easedale Tarn.

EASEDALE

A visit to Easedale Tarn has long been compulsive for those who sojourn in Grasmere. Since Victorian times, walkers have directed their steps to the tarn, leaving the Easedale road at a copse of trees where a bridge on the left over Easedale Beck takes them to a well-worn path. This leads through pastures to a steep rise alongside the descending cataract of Sourmilk Gill, to the outlet of the tarn. Suddenly a new landscape opens up: Easedale Tarn is a large expanse of pellucid water ringed by a surround of lofty fells. In pre-war days, there was an additional reward: in a hut near the outlet, an enterprising local character provided refreshments, but the hut has now fallen into ruin.

The shoreline is marshy but carries a path along which strong walkers may proceed to the inflow and continue into the upper recesses of the valley and so reach the hinterland of the Langdale Pikes. Or, by taking a path branching left, climb to the skyline near Blea Rigg and return to Grasmere by way of Silver How to complete a circular tour of rare distinction and beautiful views.

Sourmilk Gill

FAR EASEDALE

Beyond the point where the path to Easedale Tarn branches left, the road rounds a bend to enter Far Easedale, passing a few delightful residences and gardens and the start of the usual route of ascent to Helm Crag. The original path up Helm Crag has been trodden out of decent existence into a loose and slippery incline and has been recently replaced by a firmer and safer track to the top. The road becomes a rough lane alongside Easedale Beck and ends at Stythwaite Steps. Here the beck may be crossed to a rising path, where bog asphodel is rampant, that climbs steeply by the beckside into the wild upper reaches of the valley to a skyline watershed; this is marked by the few remains of a wire fence. Over the divide, the path continues around the head of the Wythburn valley and passes over another watershed before descending into Borrowdale, but this further extension of the walk should only be undertaken in clear weather and with an eye on the clock.

The heights around the upper part of Far Easedale are unfriendly and even hostile, the most fearful feature being the impending buttress of Deer Bield Crag high on the south side.

Easedale

Grisedale Hause

TONGUE GILL

Nearing Grasmere on the long descent from Dunmail Raise, the A591 reaches Mill Bridge where a signpost on the left points to the old pony route to Helvellyn. Ponies no longer come this way, but thousands of walkers do every year and, at the end of a short lane alongside a descending stream, find themselves confronted by a huge wedge that effectively divides the valley ahead into two distinct branches, each defined by a stream. This barrier is Great Tongue, and the stream descending on its left side is Little Tongue Gill and that on the right Great Tongue Gill: they meet precisely at the foot of The Tongue. The pony route elected to turn left at this impasse and climb up the grassy slope of Seat Sandal before levelling to a final stony rise to Grisedale Hause, and this is the way usually followed by pedestrians. There is also a path, easier initially, along the east side of The Tongue, but this ends in a rough scramble amongst cascades before joining the pony route for the steep climb to the Hause.

The valley of Tongue Gill is rather claustrophobic, lacking distant forward views, but having a lovely retrospect of the Vale of Grasmere as height is gained.

GREENHEAD GILL

At the Swan Hotel on the A591, a road turns down to Grasmere village, and another, soon becoming a path, leaves alongside the hotel and enters the short valley of Greenhead Gill in the company of a stream of the same name, and this may be followed up to its source on Heron Pike. But the objective of most walkers who come this way is Alcock Tarn on a shelf and reached by a steep zigzag path branching to the right and giving a bird's-eye view of the lovely Vale of Grasmere.

Grasmere churchyard

THE VALE OF GRASMERE

The Vale of Grasmere is not a separate valley as the name suggests but a brief widening of the Rothay valley where the enclosing fells are set back sufficiently to admit cultivated pastures, a lake and a village, the whole a picture of exquisite beauty perfectly arranged by nature and without blemishes other than those caused by man's intervention.

An eighteenth-century writer described Grasmere as an unsuspected paradise. A paradise it still is, at least in appearance, but no longer unsuspected: indeed, it is a place internationally known and renowned, attracting visitors from all over the world. Many come to enjoy the scenery and to walk on the fells, and many more, admirers of the writings of William Wordsworth, are drawn by the poet's associations with the village and its environs, visiting his grave in the churchyard of St Oswald's as pilgrims to a shrine, and his home at Dove Cottage where he lived with his sister Dorothy from 1799 to 1808. This is now a museum for his effects.

Wordsworth's contribution to the prosperity of the area has been immense, but he would be dismayed by the extent to which the former charm of the village has been sacrificed to commercial interests. Once a sanctuary of peace and tranquillity, there is now a constant arrival of cars and coaches almost all the year round and the streets are overrun with crowds of visitors. Where there was quiet, there is noise. Only in the depths of winter can the village be visualised as it used to be.

But the environs are as delightful as ever they were. The River Rothay curves around the churchyard, its waters crystal clear, and lingers often, loth to leave an enchanting individuality for the anonymity of the lake. Yet it is the lake with its beautiful wooded shores and solitary island that is the jewel in Grasmere's crown, happy to indulge rowing boats on its placid surface and picnic parties on its shady beaches. Pleasant walks abound and for the more active visitors, the lovely summits of Loughrigg Fell, Silver How and Helm Crag offer a permanent welcome.

The road in front of Grasmere's parish church joins the A591 at the cluster of buildings called Town End, having passed the field venue of the annual Grasmere Sports. This and a rush-bearing festival are the great local events of every year.

At the Town End junction, a minor road branches left to Dove Cottage and climbs over the brow of a hill, descending to rejoin the A591 at White Moss. This minor road was formerly the main road but is now shunned by motorists and provides an attractive pedestrian alternative, shorter and to be preferred to the new main road. It cuts a way through woodlands on bends so severe that in one section its direction is north although its aim is south.

No landscape is improved by a foreground of motor cars and at White Moss they are not only crammed into an official car park but spill on to the shores of Rydal Water, destroying both the view of this lovely lake and the peace that is its rightful heritage. White Moss is a disgrace. But by crossing a footbridge over the Rothay near the inflow and following a path through the woodland beyond, a classic view may be obtained by turning right at the top along a popular walkers' promenade which contours the slopes of Loughrigg Fell and is known to all visitors as Loughrigg Terrace. Here is seen a perfect composition, a masterpiece of nature, a beautiful and harmonious blending of lake and river, fields and fells, all arrayed in rich colours, with an overall prospect of the Vale of Grasmere and Dunmail Raise in the background. This is landscape gardening on a mammoth scale. And nowhere is there a car in sight.

The Vale of Grasmere from Loughrigg

From White Moss the main road, with a double white line down its middle, goes on to Rydal, continuous traffic permitting only glimpses of the lake alongside. A roadside rock on the right, Wordsworth's Seat, where the poet often sat as on a throne and meditated, may be seen before entering the few buildings of Rydal. Travellers on foot can avoid this busy section of road by following a path at a higher level along the side of Nab Scar.

A footbridge leaves the road on the outskirts of the village and crosses the Rothay, the river happy to be free from incarceration in the lake, and leads to a delightful path along the far shore. On the opposite side of the road is Dora's Field where, in springtime, daffodils are massed in a vivid yellow carpet. Behind this is Rydal church and Rydal Mount, Wordsworth's home from 1817 until his death in 1850. These are reached along a side road that also gives access to the fine mansion of Rydal Hall and its extensive park.

Following an appeal for funds, Rydal Mount was opened to the public in 1970 as a memorial to Wordsworth, and several of the rooms display his furniture and other effects.

Rydal Hall is now a Rest and Conference House of the Diocese of Carlisle. It was built in the sixteenth century as a residence of the Fleming family, owners of the manor, and was subsequently much altered, the imposing south range being a nineteenth-century addition. Specimen trees and the waterfalls of Rydal Beck add delight to the environs.

Rydal Water

Rydal Water from the path to Sweden Bridge

RYDALE

The side road giving access to Rydal Hall continues as a track steeply and roughly to enter the upper valley of Rydal Beck, a valley without an official name but appropriately known as Rydale. The valley is straight and long and, having no easy exit, is seldom walked although it offers a direct route to Fairfield at its head. Rydale is completely ringed by the fells forming the Fairfield Horseshoe, a popular expedition, but those who attempt this high-level marathon, despite having the valley in their sights throughout the journey, see little to invite them to make a descent, unless in emergency. In fact, Rydale is dreary, the little waterfall of Beckstones Jump being the only feature worthy of a photograph.

Near Low Sweden Bridge

FROM RYDAL, THE A591 proceeds to Ambleside, now only a long mile away, but unless there is a need to visit the town there is an opportunity to escape from the busy main road at Pelter Bridge. Here, at the south end of the village, the River Rothay may be crossed to a quiet parallel road that follows the example of the river by avoiding the town, keeping on its west bank along the base of Loughrigg Fell. This minor road runs through attractive rural surroundings with never a hint of the noise and animation of the town's streets and rejoins the main thoroughfare at Waterhead.

SCANDALE

If, however, a visit to Ambleside cannot be resisted, the A591 must be followed beyond Pelter Bridge and, now furnished with a footpath – a sure sign that a greater population is imminent – passes alongside the site of an annual sports gathering and then crosses Scandale Beck before entering Ambleside. There is little indication from the road of the valley from which the stream comes, nor any obvious access to it. The route into Scandale, for walkers only, is by way of Sweden Bridge Lane, off the Kirkstone road in the higher part of Ambleside. It leaves behind a pleasant suburbia and enters a rising lane with a fine view of the Rydal district, after which the lane passes through a delightful wood to arrive at the objective that brings most visitors into Scandale. This magnet is the ancient and picturesque High Sweden Bridge, a single span over Scandale Beck: a scene no camera can resist.

Few people go further up the valley, which is dreary in its higher reaches but carries a path over Scandale Hause into Patterdale. Instead, they prefer to return to Ambleside by taking a path on the west side of the stream, crossing it again at Low Sweden Bridge, the attraction here being the beck itself as it tumbles down a wooded gorge. Over the bridge, a tarmac lane leads back into Ambleside to complete a circular walk of a standard of beauty rare even in Lakeland.

THE CROWDS HAVE driven the charm out of Ambleside. I am sorry to have to say this; as a regular Sunday caller here for many years after the war, I had an affection for the place. I discovered a small café off the main street where, after a long day on the fells, I was served with a large plate of egg and chips and a huge pot of tea (the menu never changed) for half a crown. Almost always I was the only customer, which suited me because then I could study my map while eating. Afterwards I would make my way to the bus station for the last bus home. Things in Ambleside are not as they were. The little café has gone and there are plans to demolish the bus station and convert the site into flats. I feel a stranger to Ambleside these days.

Ambleside meets all the needs of its visitors. There are numerous shops, hotels and guest houses galore, cafés, car parks of course, even a cinema. It is a town that has happened rather than been planned, spreading out from its centre in a medley of handsome villas and terraced cottages. The buildings lack architectural distinction, the most attractive being in the older part of the town on the hillside around the old church. The newer parish church of St Mary the Virgin is handsome but

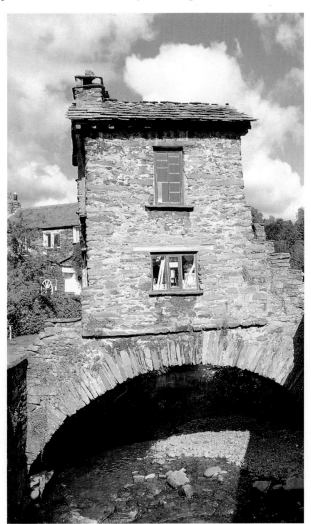

would seem more appropriate in a city street: Lakeland and church steeples don't go together. The building that most attracts attention is the quaint Bridge House, built over Stock Gill. Ambleside has turned commercial. Traffic congestion has had to be relieved by one-way streets. No longer is it a centre for quiet enjoyment and half-crown teas. Even the Rothay keeps its distance.

At the south end of the town, Waterhead, the quiet road from Pelter Bridge thrusts through another rash of hotels to join the A591. Here is the beginning of Windermere the lake (*not* Lake Windermere, please), a pier for the large passenger boats, a flotilla of yachts and small craft, water skiing, long distance swims and other aquatic sports and pastimes, picnic parties and games on the beaches, and a general air of holiday festivity. And crowds.

Adjacent is the Roman fort of *Galava*, overlooking the lake. The soldiers garrisoned here nearly two thousand years ago would be amazed at the changes that have taken place around their lonely outpost. They were conquerors, far from home and without friends. Life for them was hard. There were no festivities at Waterhead in their day.

Bridge House

Waterhead: above, *the pier and,* below, *the last ferry of the day*

Within sight of its destiny in Windermere, the Rothay welcomes the Brathay from central Lakeland and their combined waters go forward at a funeral pace, sadly aware their happy lives are coming to an end. Then they are engulfed without ceremony or requiem in the lake they have done so much to create. The bed of the Rothay valley for ten miles onwards is occupied by a lovely sheet of water in which the river loses its identity and is forgotten.

Despite overmuch exploitation for leisure pursuits and by commercial interests, Windermere remains supremely beautiful, transcending the minor irritations to which it is subjected by countless admirers. It is the most graceful of the lakes and grace is a virtue that survives and is never lost.

Main roads, always busy, closely follow the eastern shoreline to the foot of the lake at Newby Bridge. The A591 leaves Waterhead and at Low Wood, where an insensitive planning permission recently allowed a cheap building development on the lakeside, reveals a fine view across the water to the Langdale Pikes. Bordered by noble trees, the road passes the National Park Centre at Brockhole, and beyond Troutbeck Bridge reaches an insignificant but important roundabout. Here the A592 takes over as guide for the rest of the journey, soon entering and passing through Bowness-on-Windermere, so overrun by day trippers that critics prefer to call it Blackpool-on-Windermere. The parish church of St Martin, built in 1483, has witnessed its overshadowing by massive hotels and the beautiful bay it overlooks transformed to satisfy secular pleasures. Here scores of passengers can get on and off the large boats that ply along the lake, marinas and boat-building yards fringe the shore, and water speed records are attempted. The lake is the source of the local economy, the provider of Bowness's prosperity.

The A592 continues past the hotels, although more are to follow, and at Nab Wood a ferry makes the only public crossing of the lake. Then the road goes on as an avenue of trees and with glimpses of elegant residences alongside, to the end of the lake and more hotels at Newby Bridge, there joining the A590.

The western side of Windermere may also be followed, less closely but on much quieter and less direct roads and with more of interest to see along the way. Rounding the head of the lake at Waterhead and passing through Clappersgate, two left turns to the Hawkshead road make possible a detour to Wray Castle, a fine edifice but a sham with no history despite having a few mock ruins. Built in the nineteenth century as a private residence in the style of a feudal castle, it is now owned by the National Trust and used as a naval training establishment.

A few miles further, by-passing Hawkshead, is the literary Mecca of Hill Top, the home of Beatrix Potter, in the village of Near Sawrey on the road to the ferry. From the village, a road branches south for Newby Bridge soon passing the entrance to the grounds of Graythwaite Hall.

Hill Top

Stott Park Bobbin Mill   Below *Lakeside*

Graythwaite Hall, the home of the Sandys family, is an Elizabethan mansion, considerably remodelled; it stands in well-timbered grounds with open lawns and, in season, has an exotic display of rhododendrons and azaleas to which the public is admitted for a small charge that inadequately reflects the pleasure of a visit. Further on, at the corner of a road to Finsthwaite, is the Stott Park Bobbin Mill, long out of use following a decline in the demand for wooden bobbins but since restored to working order and opened as an industrial museum.

Next, the road arrives at the cottages of Lakeside, a place of summer activity with the double attraction of transport facilities for visitors wishing to embark on the big boats that ply on Windermere, calling at Bowness and Waterhead; or, from an adjacent railway station, they can revive old memories by taking a ride on a steam train on a short journey down the valley of the River Leven to Haverthwaite. For the young at heart Lakeside is exciting.

Newby Bridge

The road reaches Newby Bridge after another mile, puffs of smoke over the wall on the left side indicating the near presence of the railway.

THE VALLEY OF THE RIVER LEVEN

The main feeder of Windermere and its most generous contributor is the River Rothay but having fulfilled its function it is sunk, without trace, in the waters of the lake. Its opposite number, the outflow, emerges at the foot of the lake as the River Leven.

Without even a farewell wave, the Leven hurries away, passing in front of the Swan Hotel. Here the river is crossed by a many-arched bridge and then turns south to go hand in hand with the road and the railway to the village of Backbarrow, once industrial, with a large dolly-blue factory employing the local community: long after its closure, the bright blue footmarks of the workers to and from their homes remained on the streets, footpaths and doorsteps, and blue stains decorated the walls of the buildings. The site is now occupied by a modern hotel with time-share accommodation. A mile further, on the right, is the station and marshalling grounds of Haverthwaite on the Lakeside Railway, the only surviving part of a line from Plumpton Junction on the main coast railway; it was saved by enthusiasts whose efforts have been rewarded by a successful enterprise supported by excited children of all ages. Steam locomotives and rolling stock are on view.

Then the river leaves its companions, visits a small commercial complex, and is in turn swallowed up, the predator this time being Morecambe Bay.

GRIZEDALE FOREST

THE CONIFEROUS PLANTATIONS of the Forestry Commission in Lakeland rarely enhance the landscape and only too often are regimented dark shrouds arranged in straight lines, closely planted and starved of air and sunlight. With no regard for the instinct of the trees to grow naturally into noble specimens, they are crowded together with withered limbs, their only escape from a miserable existence in perpetual darkness being to strive upwards to the light. This is battery forestry and like all processes that deprive life of the right to live free, it is cruelty, in this case under the pretext of economic management. The Commission's aim is to grow telegraph poles, not trees.

Grizedale Forest differs from the other Grisedales in the district, which are open sheep pastures, and not only in the spelling of the name, the map-makers having presumably been deceived by the phonetic pronunciation. Things have changed dramatically in this Grizedale and the scenery has been transformed. Once it was 'back o' beyond', a secluded retreat thought fit for impounding high-ranking German prisoners of war: one escaped and was the subject of a later film *The One That Got Away*. They were interned in Grizedale Hall, since demolished.

Two developments, interlinked, have caused Grizedale's new look. The Forestry Commission, having acquired estate land, set to work with a will to cloak many miles of bare fellsides with the timber of a great forest and have succeeded well; and then, showing more sensitivity than is usual, they provided some measure of compensation to the public by opening up the forest and introducing interesting innovations of popular appeal, in which they have also succeeded well. Grizedale Hall, the country mansion that became a prison, has gone and its site provides a large car park with a lecture hall, a warden's office and a shop. There are nature trails, forest walks, picnic places, a tree nursery, a wild life museum, a camp site, an information centre, a high observation tower for the study of the birds and animals of the forest and, due to the initiative of a former Head Forester, Bill Grant, a theatre where high-class concerts are arranged and enthusiastically supported. I thought this latter project would be doomed to failure because of its remoteness from centres of population, but I have had to eat my words. In Grizedale, the Commission has shown a human face, even to the extent of preserving native trees amongst the foreigners.

At the Grizedale Visitor Centre

Satterthwaite church

Grizedale is most easily reached from Hawkshead, the road south therefrom branching at Roger Ground, the right fork climbing over Hawkshead Moor to enter the valley. Grizedale Beck has its beginnings nearby but little is seen of the stream as it descends behind a curtain of trees, and the road too becomes shrouded before reaching a complex of buildings comprising the administrative centre of the forest, the Theatre-in-the-Forest and the main concentration of visitors.

The road and the beck continue down the valley to the small village of Satterthwaite, the capital of Grizedale, encompassed by woodlands and plantations and prospering from a switch of its economy from agriculture to forestry. The neat parish church is remarkable for the beautifully executed slating of the roofs, the slates being small and laid in very narrow courses.

South of Satterthwaite, a maze of country lanes needs a map as well as signposts to ensure navigation in the direction intended. This is an area of minor undulations, shallow valleys and wandering streams, the latter all destined for Morecambe Bay and arriving there in various channels. It is a district which is entirely rural and extremely pleasant but not easily memorised; it is sparsely populated and remote from the usual haunts of tourists. People encountered here with a worried look on their faces are probably wondering where they are.

Grizedale Beck, however, has no such doubts. Sensing another valley ahead, it says goodbye to Grizedale and aims for it, arrival there being both clumsy and spectacular: the beck literally tumbles down a wooded defile choked by rocks. This exciting place is Force Falls and the valley ahead is Rusland.

Rusland is a quiet and peaceful rural backwater, so tranquil that Force Falls is quite out of character. Formerly the waters of the beck served a mill and a forge in the valley but these are now only names on a map. The most handsome residence in the valley is Rusland Hall, of seventeenth-century vintage but later enlarged, standing in a lovely garden.

The beck acquires more dignity and a new name, Rusland Pool, as it slowly makes its way down the valley to the open sea at Morecambe Bay.

Above *Force Falls*   Below *Rusland church*

YEWDALE

YEWDALE IS THE upper part of the valley occupied by Coniston Water and is encompassed on three sides by rough and craggy fells that atone for lack of height by an aggressive steepness that defies intrusion by walkers but fulfil their role as guardians and shelterers of the fertile pastures below. The road from the village of Coniston to Ambleside traverses the valley, proceeding along the west side until confronted by Holme Fell, which decisively bars the way forward; whereupon the road crosses to the east side, there rising to a watershed beyond which is the valley of Langdale. After periods of heavy rain, the facing slope of Holme Fell is delicately laced by cascading streamlets, but the main supplier of water to the valley is Yewdale Beck, issuing from Tilberthwaite Gill in an area of disused quarries. In Victorian times the gill was a showplace, its narrow gorge furnished with ladders and balconies above the rocky bed of the descending beck to permit an adventurous passage into the higher reaches of the gorge under a thin canopy of foliage to its end at an abandoned mine level. These aids to progress have gone, but Tilberthwaite Gill, reached from a signposted lane leaving the road, with Yewdale Beck alongside, is still a popular place.

A feeder of Yewdale Beck comes down alongside the road from the watershed, this entering Yew Tree Tarn, a lovely expanse of water amongst trees by the roadside and indicated by a small dam to be artificial. Another tributary nearby descends the wooded ravine of Tom Gill, where parked cars and a well-trodden path suggest there is something special to be seen. There certainly is: the path leads upwards to one of the most frequented beauty spots in Lakeland. This idyllic place is known to everybody except the Ordnance Survey as Tarn Hows, they preferring to name it The Tarns.

Yewdale Farm

Tarn Hows   Below *Boat landings on Coniston Water*

The picture that greets the eye on arriving at the outflow is as pretty as can be imagined: a delightful lake with many bays and inlets has been created by the merging of three small natural tarns artificially, the scene being set in a framework of trees and presided over by Black Fell in the background. For once, and unusually, man has rivalled nature as a bewitching landscape artist. There is road access to Tarn Hows from Hawkshead and ample car parks on arrival, all well patronised in the summer months. Fortunate indeed is the visitor who prefers to contemplate beauty undisturbed and finds himself alone at Tarn Hows.

Yewdale Beck accompanies the road down the valley but turns away on the outskirts of Coniston and enters Coniston Water.

THE CONISTON VALLEY

IN PRE-WAR DAYS, most visitors to Coniston arrived by train on a scenic railway from the south, branching from the main coastal line at Foxfield Junction. This facility was a post-war casualty, much regretted. Withdrawal of the service, however, has not lessened interest in this ex-Lancashire alpine village; on the contrary, it enjoys an increasing patronage, is catered for by shops, hotels and guest houses, and an enterprising council has provided modern amenities for the further enjoyment of visitors.

The two great natural attractions here are the Old Man and Coniston Water. The Old Man, a benevolent giant, is and has always been the village's best friend, nursing the little community in its ample lap, sheltering it from storms, and providing through the centuries the mineral wealth that has contributed so much to the local economy and prosperity before tourism brought additional rewards. The ascent of the Old Man is almost a ritual for active walkers based on Coniston, an act of homage to a veteran badly scarred by its long service to the community. Coniston Water, five straight miles in length, is served by a gondola from which passengers can admire the glorious surroundings.

Coniston Water from Brantwood

THE COPPERMINES VALLEY

In the evening shadow of the Old Man of Coniston, and quickly reached from the village, is an industrial graveyard, an area of former mining activity that has stripped the ground of all vestiges of beauty and left behind a barren wasteland of decay and devastation that even nature has not had the power to heal. This sad place has become known as Coppermines Valley. Here for centuries men laboured long hours for little reward, digging and tunnelling into the fellsides in search of the veins of copper on which their livelihood depended. Even the descending streams were made to work for a living, their main source of supply being the large tarn of Levers Water, itself brought into subjection by the building of a dam from which water was released under control. In those days there were no protests about damage to the environment, no planning prohibitions, no concern about pollution. When the mines finally closed for economic reasons, they were left to rot and decay, an unprotected

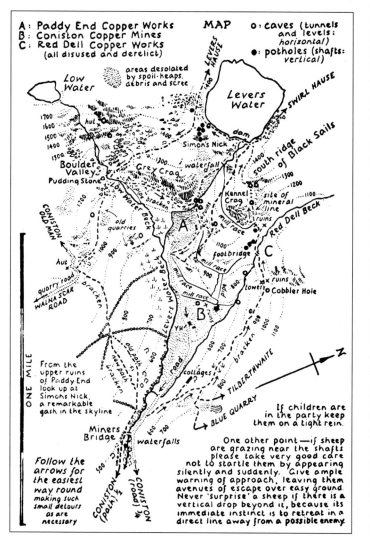

labyrinth of shafts and underground passages and a surface littered and choked with spoil from the many excavations. Buildings fell into ruin, although some were later adapted for use as a Youth Hostel, and a terrace of miners' cottages has been reprieved from collapse and given a new lease of life as holiday homes.

The Old Man suffered in silence the indignities inflicted on him by the miners, the holes they made being merely pinpricks in his massive frame. Of more concern are the great slices carved out of his sides by the slate quarries which have left him cruelly pockmarked. But looks aren't everything. He finds compensation in the admiring crowds who climb to his summit to share his exalted views of the district, and has been happy to serve the folk who chose to live in his close company.

The Coppermines Valley is reached from the village by a rising lane alongside Church Beck or by field paths to Miners Bridge. Although quite lacking in scenic charm, the sites of the mines are of absorbing interest. In the winter of 1958–59, I spent every Sunday here between buses, hunting all the levels and shafts and water cuts and workings. I append the map I made after these explorations, only to show the complexities of the area, not to induce others to visit. It is a place where dangers lurk. Some holes have been fenced but others are unprotected. Dogs and children must be kept on a tight leash and grazing sheep must not be frightened.

The Coppermines Valley

BOULDER VALLEY

The stream entering Coppermines Valley from the left has its source in Low Water, an odd name for a tarn set nearly 2000ft high, close under the summit of the Old Man. The stream, Low Water Beck, descends sharply through a hollow littered by boulders fallen from the heights above, and known locally as Boulder Valley. The largest of these scattered rocks is the Pudding Stone, a rival to the Bowder Stone in Borrowdale in dimensions and having rock-climbing routes to its top. Visitors not proficient in the sport should be content to stand and look.

The Pudding Stone

97

Brantwood

ROADS ACCOMPANY THE shores of the lake on both sides: the quieter and more pleasurable, and the one to be preferred if time is of no consequence, rounds the head of the lake and travels down the east side, never far from the water's edge and shaded throughout by native trees, outliers of a vast area of woodland. These occasionally relent to permit exquisite glimpses across the lake to its distant surround of high fells. This is a road for loitering, never for speeding. After two miles the road passes Brantwood, the home of John Ruskin. It is open to the public, and in the adjoining woods are occasional demonstrations of rural crafts and industries such as charcoal burning; on the lakeside below the terraced gardens of massed azaleas is a small jetty where the *Gondola* calls.

Beyond Brantwood the road continues as a woodland avenue, passing the scene of the tragic accident to Donald Campbell who lost his life here when his speedboat went out of control and overturned during his attempt on the water speed record in 1967. There is nothing in or on these innocent and placid waters to mark the spot, nor on the nearby shore, his memorial being in Coniston village. Further on the lake's two islands are glimpsed and the road then enters the hamlet of High Nibthwaite; here the lake receives its last tributary before narrowing to an outflowing river, the Crake.

Left behind now is the deep Coniston valley and its permanent resident, Coniston Water; left behind too is the exciting skyline of fells formed by the Old Man and his associates, and the wealth of trees, that add so much decoration to a wonderful landscape.

The road heading south out of Coniston is the village's main link with the towns of the Furness peninsula and is in regular commercial use as well as being a popular approach for seasonal holiday traffic. It leaves the village near the church as the A593 and soon passes below the site of the extinct railway station, where the ancient highway over Walna Scar, now unfit for vehicles, starts its high crossing to the Duddon valley. Further along the main road, the venerable Coniston Hall may be glimpsed on the left, grown more handsome with age, its circular chimneys a special joy: now, spanning the centuries, the Hall is a centre of camp sites and leisure facilities.

The road then swings inland, out of sight of the lake, and arrives at the small but spacious village of Torver where, with the high fells left behind and a gentler landscape ahead, the road – quieter now – branches off to Broughton-in-Furness via the Woodland valley.

Coniston Hall with its circular chimneys

Torver Falls

THE VALLEY OF TORVER BECK

The stream flowing through Torver village, not unexpectedly named Torver Beck, is here in its final stages after a long and adventurous journey from a deep mountain hollow between Dow Crag and Coniston Old Man named The Cove. The stream issues from a large tarn in a dramatic setting and careers rapidly down to pass under the Walna Scar track at Cove Bridge, still persistently named Torver Bridge on Ordnance maps. Thereafter, unable to carve a defined valley, the course of flow is across an upland wilderness badly scarred by disused quarries into one of which the stream enters in a graceful waterfall. This was an area favoured by Bronze Age settlers thousands of years ago, many of their artifacts having been found, but nobody since has shared their enthusiasm and there are no habitations. It was here too that a Kendal schoolboy won national acclaim by photographing a flying saucer as it passed overhead a few decades ago.

Only when the descending beck reaches the tree-line does it become attractive, and in a wooded dell reached by a path from the village, the placid flow of its waters is disturbed by the sudden downrush of Torver Falls.

When Torver had a railway station, pioneer rock-climbers from the towns of Furness habitually left the train here and followed Torver Beck up to their favourite climbing ground on Dow Crag, but today only a few hardy walkers do so and indeed for the ordinary rambler there is little reward in going further than Torver Falls. The flying saucers have never returned.

From the village, Torver Beck descends through fields to enter Coniston Water and the road, shed of its branch to Broughton, follows it down and continues along the lakeside. A wide opening on the right has an access road to Stable Harvey with a stream descending alongside, and offers a pleasant short diversion for walkers. A path leaves the road at a bend in the stream, this leading to the double objective of Beacon Tarn and Blawith Fell, both worthy of a leisurely visit. The main road next passes through Blawith and reaches Lowick Bridge, where it connects with the road coming down the east side of Coniston Water. The river here, the outflow of the lake, is the Crake.

THE CRAKE VALLEY

The mission of the River Crake is to carry the surplus water from Coniston's lake and deposit it in the estuary of Morecambe Bay at Greenodd. This duty it fulfils in a forthright manner, covering the five miles of the journey in an uninterrupted beeline. Roads accompany its passage on both banks, travellers on foot being well advised to keep to the east side coming from Nibthwaite; this is much quieter than the west side, which carries the A5084 with constant traffic.

The valley is shallow, flanked by rising ground of low elevation, not at all to be compared with the high fells left behind yet essentially rural in character, pretty rather than beautiful, and rather unexciting. The eastern road descends to the river at Spark Bridge where a tall mill chimney suggests that the village around is mildly industrial. Here there is a connection with the A590 main road arriving there at the ancient and interesting Farmers Arms. A mile further, the river is crossed at Penny Bridge where, on the west bank, a large and growing colony of houses is testimony to the desirable environs. In a further mile, the Crake enters the wide estuary of Greenodd Sands, an inlet of such large dimensions that its creation must be attributed to tidal waters from Morecambe Bay beyond rather than the contribution made by the river. The old village of Greenodd alongside, standing at a busy junction of roads, is now sealed off at its south end as the result of a recent bypass that follows the route of a former railway line across the sands. This, a branch from Plumpton Junction to Lakeside on Windermere, has been dismantled for much of its length but springs to life again at Haverthwaite for the last few miles of the journey.

The River Crake at Greenodd Sands

THE WOODLAND VALLEY

THE BOUNDARIES OF the Lake District National Park are arbitrary, not dictated by geographical considerations and not entirely influenced by the quality of the scenery. True, the most attractive and spectacular highlights of the area are included, but left out around the fringes are many rural backwaters free from traffic and crowds, transistor radios and commercial interests, havens of peace and solitude of individual charm and all the sweeter for being left to develop naturally without disturbance. These are the unseen gardens of Lakeland.

Such a one is the long valley draining south-west from the Coniston Fells, threaded by a quiet road linking Torver and Broughton-in-Furness and having a tiny population centred around Woodland church. Once it carried a branch railway from Foxfield Junction to Coniston on a ten-mile journey of scenic delight, where passengers did not bury their heads in newspapers but flattened their noses against the windows to see the pageant of loveliness as it passed. There was a station at Woodland but this and the railway have gone and the valley has reverted to an undisturbed calm. There is nothing in the Woodland valley to quicken the pulses. Woodland is soothing.

A lack of tarred surfaces keeps at bay motorists who like to explore without leaving their cars. The Woodland valley is for travellers on foot, walkers with a quiet appreciation and respect for unspoilt scenery.

Ranged along the east side of the valley are miniature fells, none attaining a thousand feet in height, clothed in heather and bracken, inviting, having no perils, easy of access despite an absence of paths and posing no problems of ascent. For the aged fellwalker who can no longer aspire to the Scafells and Great Gable, they are a bonus to keep him happy and in a good temper. All these minor eminences have distinctive features: Yew Bank, on the summit of Woodland Fell, has a tall and handsome obelisk that identifies it from afar; Tarn Riggs has a prehistoric cairn; Blawith Knott is a giant's grave; and the smallest named tarn in the district, Burney, has a stone circle. There are other evidences of early

occupation, in walls and piles of stones, and of more recent interest is the site of a mediaeval bloomery for the smelting of iron ore, the spoil heaps still to be seen near Green Moor Beck although nature has done its best to disguise them. The fells are interlaced by small streams running in channels that do not qualify for the status of valleys, Green Moor Beck being an exception and offering a low level route to Beacon Tarn. The main stream in the valley comes down from the high ground of Torver alongside the road, flows through the valley under the name of Kirkby Pool and then does the unexpected by turning away from its obvious destination in the Duddon Estuary to prolong its life by a long meander across the Furness peninsula, finally ending its days at Kirkby-in-Furness.

Woodland church

Broughton-in-Furness

THE LICKLE VALLEY

THE RIVER LICKLE is a Cinderella amongst Lakeland's watercourses, rarely earning a mention in guidebooks, well known to Furness folk but not at all to visitors from outside the area. Yet, in a rapid fall of almost 2000 feet from its source on White Pike in the wasteland of Torver High Common to the sands of Duddon, the river, after initially leaping down turbulently through an area devastated by large quarries, hurries along a rocky channel which is crossed by four primitive bridges, one of them an ancient clapper bridge formed by huge slabs of slate. The middle reaches, joined by tributaries, are very pleasing. Large forests of conifers cloak the fellsides, and although not to the liking of lovers of native trees they do at least soften the harsh terrain around and do not detract from the flowery banks and hedgerows alongside the rushing waters.

The area of the Lickle may be reached by a minor road from Torver built to serve the quarries, but the best starting point for a simple exploration is Broughton Mills, two miles north of Broughton-in-Furness on a quiet road. From here paths may be followed on both sides of the river, the bridges permitting a passing from one bank to the other. Evidences of antiquities will be seen on an interesting circular walk. Near Stephenson Ground on the west bank a Bronze Age settlement site is being currently excavated and two potash pits, where bracken was burnt to provide ley which was used in the manufacture of tallow and soap, can still be seen.

The Lickle discharges into the Duddon estuary near the large village of Broughton-in-Furness, its narrow streets now bypassed but still preserving many delaying attractions.

Lickle Valley

STAINTON GROUND

A narrow road turns off at Broughton Mills and climbs steadily up a side valley of the Lickle to a skyline gap. This rising hollow, watered by a small tributary of the Lickle, is commonly referred to as Stainton Ground, taking the name from one of the farms passed during the ascent. The road is normally quiet, but the top of the pass is a popular weekend halt for local motorists, an attraction being the slender summit of Stickle Pike, 1231ft, reached by a short climb to the left: it is a delectable miniature peak coveted for the garden at home, with the small Stickle Tarn nearby.

Across the road to the north are the immense disused Stainton Ground quarries, and a way through them leads to the south ridge of the much bulkier Caw, 1735ft. I was once amazed to find the cairn and triangulation column coloured a bright red, a closer inspection revealing that the stones were plastered with thousands of ladybirds, apparently resting on a migratory flight, a sight I have never seen repeated.

Over the top of the pass the road descends sharply into the Duddon valley.

THE DUDDON VALLEY

THE RIVER DUDDON is one of the most endearing watercourses in Lakeland and appropriately occupies one of the most beautiful valleys, latterly increasingly known as Dunnerdale, a name not to my liking and which I prefer not to use.

Streamlets coming down from Pike o'Blisco combine near Wrynose Pass, immediately assume the name of Duddon and flow south-west into a deepening hollow between high fells. Closely alongside is a narrow unfenced road descending from the pass; this was pioneered by the Roman invaders nearly two thousand years ago and now, with a tarmac surface but no easing of gradients, is a favourite with adventurous motorists. After two straight miles, road and river arrive at Cockley Beck where there is a farmhouse, cultivation, trees, Highland cattle and a sturdy bridge.

MOSEDALE (off Duddon Valley)

A low side valley comes down to Cockley Beck Bridge from the north-west. This is yet another Mosedale and like the others of that name is dreary and unattractive. Some maps spell it Moasdale, which is probably an aberration. The one merit of this Mosedale is that it provides the easiest crossing on foot between the Duddon valley and Eskdale. Mosedale (or Moasdale) Beck, as uninspired as its surroundings, comes down without flourishes, to join the River Duddon near Cockley Beck Bridge.

Cockley Beck near the bridge

Birks Bridge

A MOTOR ROAD crosses the bridge bound for Eskdale via Hardknott Pass. This, the most difficult car journey in the district, is a succession of hairpin bends and gradients of 1 in 3, a nerve-wracking experience for inexperienced drivers, with a black record of frustration and bad language. Even the Romans, expert road-makers, avoided this arduous climb, reaching the top of the pass by a wide detour to the south.

Without crossing the bridge at Cockley Beck, the valley road, soon becoming fenced, goes forward with the river through fertile pastures, passing isolated farmsteads and forestry cottages and, with Harter Fell looming large on the right, enters a zone of intensive plantations. This was the scene of a fire destroying many young trees, since when roadside warnings have been posted. Harter Fell, all heather and bracken when I was a lad, has since suffered a foreign invasion of conifers and now wears a dark cloak as though dressed for a funeral. Maybe it is. Maybe it is in mourning for its lost brightness and colour.

A scenic gem awaits at a bend in the road, where a lane on the right crosses the river at Birks Bridge. From the west bank a few yards downstream, the bridge is seen as a graceful arch high above a bed of pebbles caressed by crystal-clear waters. Again one is left wondering why the builders of centuries ago were so much more adept at applying their skills than those of today: they were artists as well as craftsmen, marrying their works to the environs.

The road goes on through more open country, passing the little settlement of Troutal, beyond which a footpath on the right leads through fields to the river at Fickle Steps. Here a line of large boulders enable sure-footed pedestrians to cross dryshod to the far bank where a track climbs amongst trees to Grassguards, joining another that goes over a depression into Eskdale. The boulders need caution – those with unsteady legs risk a wetting – but even the unfortunates who suffer a misadventure will agree that the crossing is an idyllic section of the river.

Resuming the road, cross Seathwaite Bridge and continue forward by a lively stream, wrongly assumed by casual visitors to be the Duddon; this, however, is out of sight amongst woodlands on the right. The stream now alongside is Tarn Beck.

THE VALLEY OF TARN BECK

Tarn Beck has its origins in Seathwaite Tarn, a large sheet of water lying in a fold of the fells between Grey Friar and Dow Crag. Near the head of the tarn are some disused mines and the foot is closed by a dam, confirming its use as a reservoir. There is little of interest here or along the issuing beck or the access road as they go down to the main valley, but below Seathwaite Bridge, after passing a road leaving for Walna Scar, the beck blossoms into exquisite beauty, cascading and tree-fringed, as it hurries with the road to the sweet hamlet of Seathwaite.

Bridge over Tarn Beck Below *Tarn Beck*

Seathwaite church

SEATHWAITE IS THE largest settlement in the Duddon valley but there is very little of it: a church, an inn, a few cottages and barns, yet it holds a fond place in memory. Many are the times I have ended a hard walk here, been refreshed at a tea-room near the inn, and waited for the Saturday bus to come up the valley, turn around and take me to Ulverston to join another bus home.

Seathwaite's best known resident was the Rev. Robert Walker, curate of the church for sixty-seven years, who became a celebrity through the writings of Wordsworth. After a life of self denial that earned him the name of Wonderful Walker, he died in 1802 at the age of ninety-three and was buried under a yew tree.

Charming walks abound in the vicinity of Seathwaite, the most frequented being to Wallowbarrow Gorge, a tremendous rift of Himalayan proportions through which the River Duddon races amid scenes of wild disarray softened by trees. The path to this remarkable place leaves the road opposite the church and passes through a woodland where Tarn Beck is crossed on its way to join the river, and reaches the gorge at a fine bridge, new since my time. From here a path can be followed up to Grassguards and over into Eskdale.

Near Wallowbarrow

Ulpha Bridge

Round a corner at Seathwaite, the road heads seawards and the river, released from the confines of Wallowbarrow Gorge, flows more placidly through fields on the right in gentler surroundings, both reaching the farming complex of Hall Dunnerdale. Here the narrow road to Broughton Mills starts its long climb and the river is crossed to its west bank. The next habitations are at Ulpha, a scattered village of disputed origin, but thought to have roots in Celtic times. A steep road branches off to cross the moors to Eskdale, the main road re-crossing the river alongside Ulpha church.

Finally, the road runs high along the side of Dunnerdale Fells, a group of minor heights that may be explored by following a path in the company of a descending stream opposite the solitary buildings of Stonestar, before descending sharply to the busy coastal road, the A595, at Duddon Bridge, Broughton-in-Furness being a mile to the left. Amongst the trees on the west bank of the river hereabouts is the preserved site of an old bloomery or furnace where iron ore was smelted by charcoal from nearby coppice woods.

Duddon Bridge accommodates the widening bed of the river as it enters the great estuary it has formed aided and abetted by the tidal waters of the Irish Sea. Here the River Duddon bids a sad farewell to its lovely valley and ends a journey at times exciting and everywhere beautiful.

PART THREE

The Western Valleys

Harter Fell from Penny Hill
Left Scafells from Throstle Garth

ESKDALE

IN SOME RESPECTS Eskdale and the Duddon valley are identical twins, the charming offspring of a close-knit family of giants forming the high central mass of Lakeland. Born in a harsh wilderness of rock and scree, and savaged by storms, both valleys come of rough stock and are initially uncouth and unattractive, but as they take shape they gradually contrive to introduce elements of beauty, so successfully indeed that in maturity they lay carpets of colour all the way to the coast. Both valleys carry rivers of sparkling purity that nourish fertile pastures and woodlands as they aim resolutely for the open sea. Both valleys are served by roads, but here there is a point of difference: the Duddon valley has a through road and can be traversed by cars from end to end, entry commonly being made at the head, Wrynose Pass, but the road in Eskdale has easy access only from the coast, and in mid-valley escapes to avoid confrontation with a mountain barrier ahead: upper Eskdale is an exclusive preserve of travellers on foot.

Both valleys trend south-west from their sources, at first roughly parallel, but Eskdale slowly changes course and drifts away due west: the outflows of their rivers are a dozen miles apart, the intervening distance being occupied by the massive headland of Black Combe. This was left out in the cold by the definers of the National Park and is reluctantly omitted from this book for considerations of space.

Muncaster Castle

Low tide at Ravenglass

The River Esk ends its days on the coast at Eskmeals and in its death throes is a writhing serpent struggling against gravity and evidently loth to leave the valley for the open sea. Its final tortuous channel is a long estuary crossed by the main line railway and at its head by the main road, the A595. Purists determined to travel the valley throughout can leave the bridge by an unclassified road to Eskdale Green but the majority who intend to visit only the highlights of Eskdale invariably continue to Ravenglass, climbing over a hill dominated by the embattled pile of Muncaster Castle. Here a large roadside car park is an invitation to visit the lovely grounds of the castle and, in season, an exotic display of rhododendrons and azaleas. Beyond the castle entrance, the road descends to a junction where a branch continues downhill to the fishing village of Ravenglass.

Ravenglass was known to the Roman invaders a thousand years before the native Britons settled here, and was a key point in their conquest of the north-west. Here they built a fort, of which little remains to be seen, and from it they engineered a road through the fells to another at Ambleside known as *Galava*. They have, however, left as evidence of their occupation a bath-house that has survived the centuries remarkably well: this antiquity, sometimes referred to as Walls Castle, and possibly alternatively occupied as a villa, is found alongside a leafy lane near the railway station and adjacent to the fort but divided from it by the railway line, no respecter of ancient relics.

Ravenglass is interesting. Rows of cottages and an excellent hotel line the sides of a main street that ends in a ramp sloping down to the waters of an estuary with the open sea in sight ahead. Small craft and screaming seagulls add a nautical touch to the moorings but Ravenglass has no pretensions as a port although the Romans and others since have found it a safe harbour. The estuary is that of the River Mite, not that of the Esk as is often supposed by casual visitors, and across it are the interminable sand dunes of Drigg.

But the crowds who come to Ravenglass do so not to see the main street or the estuary or the Roman remains. They go to the railway station where a special attraction awaits.

Ravenglass Railway Station

The focal point of attention on Ravenglass Railway Station is centred not on the main platforms but on a side bay where miniature steam locomotives pull in on a narrow gauge track with a tailback of open carriages which stand waiting, proud and dignified in resplendent livery, and quite disdainful of the massive diesels on the main line. They, the midgets, are the object of admiration, not the leviathans, and they know it. Small is beautiful on Ravenglass Station.

'All aboard for Eskdale' is a command that sends waiting juveniles into frenzies of excitement, sets mature hearts pounding, and turns old men into little boys again. They are about to start a seven-mile journey of sheer delight, a unique experience they will always remember and want to repeat often. The little engines, too, strain at the leash, eager to be off and show their prowess. Their mission is to give pleasure to their patrons, and right well they succeed.

The Ravenglass and Eskdale Railway, affectionately known as Ratty, has suffered and enjoyed many changes of fortune and many changes of management since the line was opened in 1875 to serve the iron mines in Eskdale; when the mines closed, the railway was used for the transport of granite from the adjacent quarries. Local people were allowed to travel as passengers, and goods were carried. Changes were made during a troubled history. In 1915, the original 3-foot gauge was replaced by the present 15-inch. Bad times followed. There were closures, suspensions and bankruptcies. The railway was saved from extinction by its friends in 1960, when an appeal for funds and much attendant publicity resulted in its purchase at auction for £12,000. A complete overhaul was then undertaken, new rolling stock acquired, passenger facilities provided, and finally with everything in pristine condition the line was opened to the public and the willing hands of enthusiasts rewarded for their enterprise by a highly popular and successful attraction. Li'l Ratty has become greatly loved.

Amid puffs of steam and whoops of joy, the little train departs with the eagerness of a terrier chasing a rabbit, crossing over the road and passing the engine sheds and workshops to enter a marshy hollow. There are open views ahead to an exciting skyline formed by the high western fells of Lakeland, while the River Mite is in attendance. The line then passes under the A595 and arrives at its first halt at a complex of buildings. This is Muncaster Mill, a fifteenth-century water-powered corn mill saved from dereliction by the owners of the railway and, greatly to their credit, renovated and restored to working order, the repaired water wheel and mill race adding interest to the journey.

114

Now the brave little engine faces a three-mile incline to Irton Road Station along the side of Muncaster Fell. The valley followed thus far is Miterdale, the lower reaches of Eskdale being concealed by the fell, but soon this barrier is rounded on a downhill gradient into Eskdale and there is a first sighting of the River Esk. The place of arrival is Eskdale Green Station in a pleasant scattered community where roads come in from the A595 to Eskmeals and over the moorland from Ulpha in the Duddon valley. Eskdale Green has an inn which demonstrated its loyalty by changing it name from the King of Prussia to the King George at the outbreak of the war in 1914; nearby is an Outward Bound School with an excellent record of service to deprived youngsters from the towns and cities. From here too Miterdale, a shy and hidden valley, may be explored on foot.

MITERDALE

As a diversion on a visit to Eskdale, a ramble to the head of Miterdale can be recommended to walkers who prefer solitude to crowds. Passengers on the train from Ravenglass have already travelled the lower four miles of this valley but depart from it when the line curves down to Eskdale Green Station. A rising lane from the station rejoins the River Mite, which may then be followed up past farm buildings to a surprising climax where a final amphitheatre is surrounded by a ring of cliffs falling from the upland shelf containing Burnmoor Tarn with Scafell rising grandly beyond. This is a scene without a counterpart in Lakeland.

The head of Miterdale

Li'l Ratty arrives at Dalegarth Station

RESUMING THE TRAIN journey at Eskdale Green, a mile-long leafy cutting, bright with flowers and blossom, leads to a final curve and the end of the line at Dalegarth Station. The original track continued straight ahead to the iron mines near the village of Boot but the gradient was too much for the narrow gauge laid later and the line was then diverted to a new terminus alongside the valley road, where a shop and café and facilities for passengers were incorporated subsequently. Passengers disembark at Dalegarth Station reluctantly but consoled by the prospect of the return journey still to come. As they leave the station, they form two processions along the road, one party heading to sample the few fleshpots of Boot, the others directed by signposts to Dalegarth Force.

Dalegarth Force, falling in a single graceful leap of sixty feet in a wooded ravine, is a spectacle of such beauty that the early guidebook writers were unanimous in describing it as the finest waterfall in Lakeland. Victorian sightseers paid for the privilege of witnessing this superb scene but access today is free and the walk may be extended above the fall by paths and bridges: this is a short but delightful expedition that makes a visitor feel sorry for those who opted to spend the time between trains at Boot.

Boot is a small village yet it has the largest concentration of buildings in Eskdale and as the centre of an extensive parish exercises authority over a wide area. Its development has been subject to many influences. Evidences of Neolithic and Bronze Age occupation have been found on the nearby fellsides but with the dawn of recorded history came the first primitive settlers to farm the land. Then for three centuries the Romans were masters in the valley, establishing communications between the port of Ravenglass and their great fort at Hardknott, and operating the iron ore mines. Later the feudal overlords of the Barony of Eskdale and the monks of Furness Abbey contributed to the development of the valley by the introduction of new techniques of farming and corn milling. But the evolution of Boot as a settled community was mainly due to the exploitation of the iron mines. Miners' cottages were built and narrow lanes made for the passage of horses and carts. Little has changed. Boot looks its age. It belongs to times long gone. Many of the cottages are now holiday homes and annexes of the local inn, but not even the advent of tourism, encouraged by the railway, has altered the character of the village. It is content to remain as it has always been. Progress is a foreign word.

The most interesting surviving relic of bygone days is the water-powered corn mill alongside the tumbling cascades of Whillan Beck, thought to be a replacement of a thirteenth-century mill on the same site. It was happily preserved and restored by Cumbria County Council in 1975.

THE VALLEY OF WHILLAN BECK

The corn mill is reached over a packhorse bridge at the extremity of the village. Whillan Beck here is delightful and may be followed on a path upstream for some distance. To follow it to its source is a much longer expedition. Over the packhorse bridge, a rough path climbs steeply with the old iron mines and the track of the original railway seen on the left. Then it turns away above the stream on a gradual climb of three miles to Burnmoor Tarn, the stream rising nearby on the right all the way to its outlet from the tarn. Here there is a topographical curiosity: what appears, at first glance, to be an impossibility. Although the tarn is very large, with the proportions of a lake, the issuing stream, Whillan Beck, is almost alongside and only a few paces distant from the entering stream, Hardrigg Gill, and there is no apparent change of contour between them. Decidedly odd! Nature seems to have suffered an aberration at Burnmoor Tarn.

The path thus far, and which continues over into Wasdale, was in former days a corpse road along which, before there was consecrated ground at Wasdale Head, the bodies of the dead were conveyed on horseback to Boot for interment.

The corn mill and packhorse bridge at Boot

THE ESKDALE VALLEY road skirts Boot without entering the village and continues alongside a wood to reach the Woolpack Inn. Progress along Eskdale is often delayed by tempting diversion, and behind the inn a waymarked rising path leads up to Eel Tarn, one of the most charming with its floating carpet of water lilies. The road goes on past the Woolpack and the Eskdale Youth Hostel; the river is on the right but at Whahouse Bridge crosses it and heads directly through fields to reach the foot of Hardknott Pass at a popular halt where Hardknott Gill passes under the road to join the river. Motorists can go no further up the valley of the River Esk; here they may turn back or face the hazards of Hardknott Pass which, if negotiated safely, will take them over the skyline to Cockley Beck in the Duddon valley and two choices of escape.

Visitors not encumbered by cars can reach the bridge at the foot of Hardknott Pass from Boot by a longer but exceedingly pleasant alternative. A lane branching off the road opposite the village goes down to the humble seventeenth-century parish church of St Catherine, a plain structure but having in its churchyard an ornately carved headstone over the grave of Tommy Dobson, one time Master of the Eskdale Foxhounds. Tommy's name has not lived on as has John Peel's yet he was held in equal esteem locally. The headstone, lovingly embellished not with cherubs and angels, but with his own effigy and the symbols of hunting, is a work of art, a wonderful tribute not only to Tommy but also to the skill of the craftsman who executed it.

Beyond the church is the River Esk and a path turns alongside and leads upstream in idyllic surroundings to Doctor Bridge, where the main road may be regained near the Woolpack Inn by a short lane. Preferably, however, the farm road to Penny Hill Farm directly ahead should be followed with the river now on the left. Past the farm, a path turns up the fellside bound for Harter Fell and the Duddon valley, but by continuing without deflection in the amiable company of the tree-lined river, the bridge at the foot of Hardknott Pass will be reached.

From this point, both wheels and boots climb the steep road towards the pass for half a mile until abreast of the site of the great Roman fort at *Mediobocdum*, better known and more easily pronounced as Hardknott Castle.

Boot church	*The grave of Tommy Dobson*

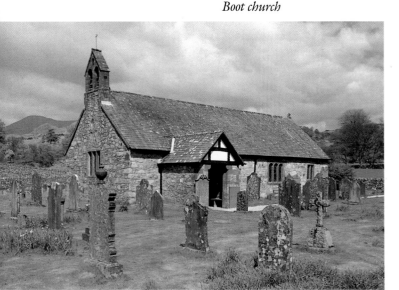

The Scafells from the north gate of Hard Knott fort

Hard Knott is the rugged height overlooking and dominating the pass to which it has given its name. The south-western slopes fall steeply from the cliffs of Border End to an inclined grassy shelf extending for half a mile before breaking abruptly in a line of crags above the valley of the Esk. This shelf, a strategic place of vantage commanding a view of Eskdale from the mountains to the coast, was selected by the Romans towards the end of the first century AD as a site for establishing a garrison to reinforce their military occupation of the district, and here they built their largest fort. Although now ruinous, the main structure and outbuildings have survived the passing of time sufficiently to yield much valuable information.

In recent years the walls of the fort were rebuilt by the Ministry of Works, a slate course indicating the original wall below and the restored part above. There is divided opinion as to whether this physical reconstruction is desirable. Would not the ruins, left to natural decay, have had a greater stimulus to the imagination? English Heritage, who now care for the site, please note.

The ruins of Hard Knott fort

Throstle Garth

The upper part of Eskdale is a closed shop for motorists who prefer not to wander out of sight of their cars. This is wild terrain without roads, an area of steep ups and downs where the fells assume the proportions of mountains. The Scafells, Bowfell and Crinkle Crags close the valley abruptly and brutally by a barrier of crags and stony declivities that show no mercy to tired limbs; there are no habitations, no refuges. To follow the valley up to its beginnings is an arduous climb, not to be undertaken lightly and only by experienced fellwalkers. Weaklings, keep away.

At the foot of Hardknott Pass an access lane leads to the farm of Brotherilkeld and continues as an easy path with the Esk an amiable companion for two miles in a narrowing valley between Heron Crag on the left and Yew Crags on the right, while Bowfell is a graceful pyramid ahead. At a confluence of waters, Lingcove Bridge is reached, this ancient arch spanning Lingcove Beck as it tumbles in waterfalls to join the Esk; a rough path climbs alongside bound for Great Langdale by way of Three Tarns. At the bridge, the River Esk comes in from the left and is followed by crossing the bridge to a rising path high above the river, which here leaps along a narrow channel, earning the name of Esk Falls. Now seen directly ahead are the neighbouring giants of Scafell Pike and Ill Crag. This exciting place is Throstle Garth.

Those unaccustomed to rough walking are advised to turn back at Lingcove Bridge and return the way they came and find compensation for their default in a paddle in one of the many inviting pools in the river bed. Only strong walkers should seek to penetrate the upper recesses of the valley to its extremity and even they should think twice if they have to be at Dalegarth to catch the last train. Used as a through route to Wasdale, Borrowdale or Langdale, the upper valley is a challenge for the very fit, but this is inhospitable territory and parties attempting this arduous expedition have been benighted here.

Those determined to press on, come what may, follow the path from Lingcove Bridge and arrive with the river at a flat tract of marshy ground, Great Moss, where the waterfall of Cam Spout joins the river from the heights of Scafell Pike, towering behind, with an ascending path alongside. Great Moss is thought to have been a deer park of the monks of Furness Abbey.

Here the river again changes direction coming down from the north, and is kept alongside below the cliffs of Dow Crag, also known as Esk Buttress to distinguish it from the better known Dow Crag near Coniston. Beyond, a stream comes down from Little Narrowcove, better described as a ravine than a valley: this offers an unorthodox route to Scafell Pike below the beetling rocks of Ill Crag, and presents an aspect of the Pike that will surprise the majority who approach it from Esk Hause.

Continuing alongside the infant Esk, a stream, Calfcove Gill, joins in and the final stage is a pathless scramble up The Tongue between the two to reach the high saddle of Esk Hause at 2490ft, with a glorious prospect over Borrowdale ahead.

Esk Hause is the end, or strictly the beginning of Eskdale, one of the grandest of Lakeland's valleys, a succession of dramatic landscapes ranged around a lovely river. All good things come to an end but in Eskdale not until the very last step is taken to set foot on Esk Hause.

Scafell Pike from the River Esk

Bowfell at the head of Eskdale

WASDALE (*in Cumberland*)

THE COASTAL ROAD, A595, leaves Muncaster and crosses the miniature railway and the River Mite. Just after the village of Holmrook, a minor road on the right leads to the threshold of Wasdale, a valley hardly known to the tourists of a century ago but which has since been established as the premier centre in Lakeland for rock-climbers, hardy and adventurous fellwalkers and admirers of mountain grandeur, most of the activity being centred at the head of the valley. This remote hollow, a green oasis encircled by gaunt mountains, was 'discovered' towards the end of the last century, mainly by professional men from the cities who escaped from their urban environments to find freedom and exercise and thrilling adventure in exploring the virgin heights around. They were the pioneers of rock-climbing in the district and, joined by local enthusiasts, formed The Fell and Rock Climbing Club of the English Lake District.

The Club's base of operations and meeting place was the Wasdale Head Inn. At that time, the inn had as its landlord a remarkable character, Will Ritson, a practical joker and philosopher, rough in speech but not at all overawed by his erudite guests. He used to boast that Wasdale had the highest mountain, the deepest lake and the biggest liar in the country, the latter himself. He was sceptical of the exploits of his visitors; when told of their intention to climb the crags of Scafell he dismissed the idea, saying 'nobbut a fleeing thing could get up theer'. But they proved him wrong, and as their exploits gained national publicity, supplemented by the wonderfully detailed photographs of the Abraham Brothers of Keswick, interest in the new sport of rock-climbing developed rapidly. The atmosphere of the inn in those early years was quite extraordinary, lacking decorum and polite manners. When I first went there, after Ritson's day, the entrance hall was choked with climbing ropes, heavy boots and drying clothes, the guests were all served at one large table in a room decorated by pictures, all of crags and climbers in action supplied by the Abrahams, the talk was all of the day's activities. The evenings were opportunities to practise techniques on the stairs and furniture, or on the walls of the outbuildings – what fun we had.

But those days are over and the former atmosphere of the inn has gone forever. Guests no longer arrive on foot or by ponycart from the nearest railway station at Drigg as the earliest visitors did. Sophistication has set in. The coming of the car changed all that. People are now driven to the door of the inn in cars and coaches, and disembark wearing sandals and skirts, T-shirts and shorts, and make for the bar without a glance at the magnificent array of peaks around. The inn, happily, has reverted to its original name after announcing itself as the Wastwater Hotel for many years, but what's in a name? The old happy days are gone forever.

Left *Great Gable from Wasdale Head*
Right *Wasdale Head Inn*

Nether Wasdale

The road leaving the A595 for Santon Bridge heads north-east in attractive scenery akin to that of a rural shire. In the first few miles there is no hint of the excitements that lie in wait ahead. The tree-lined road affords glimpses of farmsteads along the way and the River Irt on the right, with occasional sighting of bordering fells of low stature yet sufficiently elevated to assure travellers that they are entering a valley. Past Santon Bridge, with the river now away to the left, the area of Nether Wasdale is reached and is entirely agricultural; the small village of Strands is reached by a road branching left. Beyond this junction, opposite Woodhow Farm, a path goes down to the river, crossing it at Lund Bridge to gain access to the gravelly flats where the Irt issues in sinuous curves from the lake of Wastwater, here revealed ahead. This is a placid spot, with a distant background of mountains and only the nearby steep slopes of Whin Rigg plunging in disarray to the water's edge suggesting that the further reaches of the valley may not be quite as peaceful.

With views restricted by the wooded grounds of Wasdale Hall, the road along the side of Wastwater goes on to emerge from the trees into a naked and savage landscape with a suddenness that stuns the senses. The transformation is instantaneous and complete: behind now are the sylvan delights of Nether Wasdale; ahead, in a blinding revelation, is a scene almost brutal in its wildness and desolation. Wastwater, deepest of the lakes, is now seen fully as a curving black expanse of evil appearance, its sinister aspect emphasised by a shattered backcloth of rocks and scree falling steeply into the dark waters from a fractured rim of crags nearly two thousand feet above. An arid curtain of stones extends far into the distance from the horrendous cliffs and gullies of Whin Rigg directly opposite.

Wastwater Screes are tremendously impressive, a petrified downfall of debris without life or movement yet seeming to imaginative observers to pose a threat to continued progress along the road. I have known visitors turn back, fearful and vowing never to return.

With the head of the valley now in sight, although distantly, the road leads towards it, now narrow and unenclosed and skirting the shoreline so intimately that nervous car drivers may well suffer qualms. Along here there is a grandstand view of the screes across the dark waters of the lake, seemingly hostile and unapproachable although actually having a path above the water's edge that poses no difficulties except at one section where for a hundred yards pedestrians must clamber like monkeys over huge boulders.

Wastwater Screes, normally harsh and intimidating, have moments of beauty when the setting sun diffuses the stony wastes in a rosy glow.

Wastwater Screes

A mile along the lakeside, the road is joined by another coming from Gosforth along the base of the line of fells that define the western boundary of Wasdale and is seen to be breached by a channel bringing down a stream from the unfrequented hinterland of Copeland Forest. This is Greendale Gill.

GREENDALE

Although named as a dale, the valley of Greendale is hardly more than a rough watercourse with little of immediate interest. A path climbs alongside the descending stream and arrives at its source in Greendale Tarn, lying in a hollow between the heights of Seatallan and Middle Fell. The tarn has no special beauty to add to a barren landscape. Anglers may find some appeal in its sullen waters, but for walkers Greendale's one merit is the access offered to the moorland wilderness beyond. It is no place for picnics.

FROM THE JUNCTION, the road to Wasdale Head continues as before, skirting the shore of Wastwater. At one point, a rocky promontory thrusts into the lake, providing a perch for visitors not too overawed by the grim surroundings, and gives an uninterrupted view to the mountains that bring the valley to an abrupt end.

Further along the road a clump of trees is a welcome oasis. Here, within a short distance, Netherbeck Bridge and Overbeck Bridge cross streams coming down from the left to augment Wastwater under the stern supervision of Yewbarrow, a fell rising immediately beyond.

The Scafells from Wastwater

Nether Beck with Yewbarrow behind

THE VALLEY OF NETHER BECK

Like the neighbouring Greendale, Nether Beck comes down a narrow cutting from its source in a tarn high amongst the fells and has a path alongside, but it lacks the usual pleasantries of trees and green pastures. The initial approaches are attractive, however, the beck leaping in a series of waterfalls. It issues from Scoat Tarn at an altitude of 1956ft, a place much favoured by trout fishermen.

BOWDERDALE

Bowderdale is the valley of Over Beck, forming the rising western boundary of Yewbarrow but having little to deserve appreciative comment. Bowderdale Farm and the beck, both reached from Overbeck Bridge, are the only permanent institutions in a valley devoid of other interest. The beck may be followed up to its source at Dore Head where further easy progress is halted by a steep and arduous scree run falling into Mosedale. The valley thus far does, however, offer the easiest approach to the Mosedale Horseshoe, an exhilarating mountain marathon for experienced fellwalkers only.

Netherbeck Bridge

The packhorse bridge at Wasdale Head

BEYOND OVERBECK BRIDGE, the road runs alongside the slopes of Yewbarrow and provides a momentary sighting of the thrones of the gods, Scafell and Scafell Pike, the highest ground in England, poised against the sky above the ravine of Lingmell Gill: this is a violent eruption contrasting with the smooth waters of the lake in the foreground.

Lingmell Gill was made impassable by a pre-war cloudburst that brought down an avalanche of boulders from the mountains above and choked the ravine, spilling over the pastures at the head of the lake, but it was later cleared by German prisoners. Access to the gill is made at mid-height by a rising path from the valley further along, this being the popular route to the Scafells from Wasdale Head.

The head of the lake is soon reached and skirted by a lane that gives access to the farm of Wasdale Head Hall where the path along the base of the Screes commences. There is access also to Brackenclose, the home of the Fell and Rock Climbing Club, and to the old corpse road to Boot via Burnmoor Tarn.

The road, now in its final stages, crosses Mosedale Beck and enters a green bowl patterned by sturdy stone walls and tightly ringed by lofty mountains. A little group of buildings ahead signals the end of civilisation. This is Wasdale Head.

Standing outside the inn, it is easy for a redblooded observer to appreciate the compelling effect of the surroundings on the adventurous Victorians who came here year after year. It was their exploits on the fells and crags, recorded for posterity, which put Wasdale Head firmly on the agenda of the generations of walkers and climbers who have followed in their footsteps and handholds.

The packhorse bridge, looking up towards Pillar

Great Gable towers magnificently over the valley, its tapering pyramid and girdle offering an irresistible challenge; Kirk Fell is a treadmill to heaven, and Lingmell directly opposite is a shield defending the Scafells behind. From the old packhorse bridge over Mosedale Beck at the rear of the inn, the high skyline of the Pillar range promises an excellent expedition, and Yewbarrow, soaring directly not only protects the little community from westerly gales but is a fine viewpoint with surveillance over the whole valley.

There is no other place with the magnetism of Wasdale Head.

Short walks in the vicinity that can be undertaken before toes start turning upwards are few, but a stroll to the tiny church hidden by a screen of trees across the fields should certainly be made. Here are graveyard memories of climbers who ventured too far, and look for the window that has an engraving of Napes Needle on Great Gable. Ritson surprisingly did not include the smallest church in England in his list of the unique attributes of Wasdale; perhaps his guests assured him otherwise.

There appears to be no route of escape from Wasdale Head other than by way of the approach road, the barrier of fells being unbroken, but unseen are two pedestrian paths, one crossing Black Sail Pass into Ennerdale and the other passing over Sty Head for Borrowdale or Langdale. Both involve a considerable amount of rough climbing and neither is suitable for those who prefer to potter in the valleys.

Two streams, Mosedale Beck and Lingmell Beck, enter the valley from hidden recesses, both hurrying to join Wastwater and issuing from side valleys that can be penetrated without encountering difficulties and which have features of interest.

129

Mosedale

MOSEDALE

This Mosedale is the most impressive of the many of that name. A path leaves the bridge behind the inn and rises through pastures along the base of Yewbarrow with Mosedale Beck descending on the right; trees hide the shy waterfall of Ritson's Force. Beyond the domain of Yewbarrow, the path crosses the bottom of the scree run which litters the slope below Dore Head: this has a reputation as the worst scree run in the district and it gets worse each year as descending walkers trample the verges to secure a firmer footing on the slippery slope. In scenes of increasing wilderness, the path continues along the floor of the valley with the beck in close attendance; the steep, scarred slopes of Red Pike, a shadowy no-man's-land, is of threatening aspect. A large fallen block split by a Y-shaped crack was known as the Y-boulder to the early rock-climbers and provided much sport, the test being to climb it feet first.

The valley ends in a lonely recess when confronted by the tiered crags of Blackem (Black Comb) Head. This is a wild place with no evidence that others have been here before, the profound silence broken only by the trickle of water draining from the rocks. But even on this sterile ground, beauty blushes unseen and undisturbed; the marshy hollows and crevices have been colonised by the starry saxifrage in a gallant attempt to transform desolation into a garden. It is a pity that nobody comes to admire their charming display.

Mosedale Beck, near Ritson's Force

THE VALLEY OF LINGMELL BECK

The last buildings at Wasdale Head are at the farm of Burnthwaite, reached by a lane that bears the imprints of hundreds of boots on almost every day of every year since this is a much-trodden approach to a popular walkers' crossroads at Sty Head Pass. Beyond the farm, two routes are available: the modern version is a blazed track rising along the flank of Great Gable but this has degenerated through overuse into a stony and ugly scar; the other and original route, now neglected and infinitely more pleasurable, keeps alongside the descending Lingmell Beck and Spouthead Gill to a final grassy rise to the pass.

This latter route was known to early visitors as the Valley Route. At a beautiful watersmeet a stream from Lingmell joins in, and this, followed upwards, leads to the great rift of Piers Gill; this is Lakeland's own Grand Canyon, a tremendous cleft between high vertical walls of rock. The portals may be entered but progress is soon barred by an impassable waterfall. There is no way through and those who think there is soon come to grief. Turn back to the safety of Wasdale Head with a last lingering look at Great Gable. There is nothing like this back at home.

Heaven forfend that Wasdale should ever fall prey to timeshare operators and commercial developers, or to the Forestry Commission. Ten years ago British Nuclear Fuels, who already take water from the River Irt, proposed to raise the level of Wastwater by constructing a weir at the outflow and abstract more water but were defeated by a spirited opposition from Wasdale's many friends and sent home to Sellafield with a bloody nose. This should be the fate of all intending predators. Wasdale is too precious to be exploited for profit. It is a surviving reminder of Lakeland as it used to be in the happy days before the spoilers came. There is no welcome in Wasdale for Big Brothers.

Wasdale Head from Lingmell

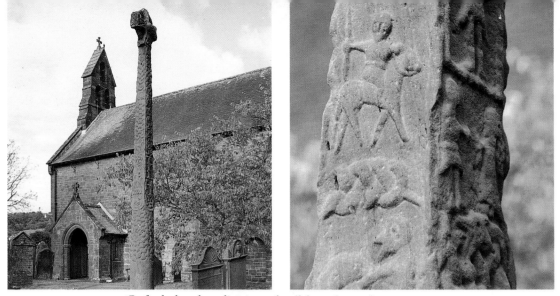

Gosforth church and, right, *a detail from the tenth-century cross*

BLENGDALE

THE NEXT VALLEY reached along the A595 after passing the entrance to Wasdale is indicated by the crossing of the River Bleng at Gosforth and is totally different in character and appearance, having no grand mountains to give it an air of majesty, no lake and very few visitors. There was a time when following the river up to its source was a convenient way of reaching the high fells along the southern border of Ennerdale: this was a lonely journey into an upland wilderness with no paths, no habitations and little prospect of meeting other walkers. The only merits of this trek were the easy gradients with no serious climbing and the ultimate reward on reaching the ridge of a glorious view of the central heights of Lakeland over the deep trench of Ennerdale. There was little to excite interest along the way and, with the river as guide, there was no problem in route-finding.

But in the last few decades Blengdale has been transformed. The Forestry Commission have taken it over in a big way and the middle reaches are cloaked by vast plantations of conifers that form a barrier to the bare upper slopes. Walkers who walk for pleasure will find little of it in threading their way through the dark avenues, and lovers of trees will be saddened at the sight of so many unable to grow freely and losing their instinct to live. For those who find joy in nature, Blengdale is a write-off.

Several streamlets drain from the Ennerdale ridge and unite to form the River Bleng which then heads south-west on a ten-mile journey to the sea, passing initially along declining fellsides without incident until confronted by the dense plantations of the forest. When abreast of the trees, the open Stockdale Moor on the right has excitements for the antiquarian: here is the site of an ancient British settlement with tumuli and cairns and enclosures to prove it, and beyond is a tumble of boulders known as Sampson's Bratfull. The river, undeterred by the new environment that has encompassed it in the last half-century, makes its way through the forest area as though nothing had happened and emerges into open daylight at Wellington Bridge, carrying a road to Wasdale Head, and then bypasses the attractive village of Gosforth a mile further on. After this it flows on a reluctant final stage to the sea, sharing its death throes with the River Irt.

Gosforth, happily situated off the busy main road, is too good to miss. There are some interesting old buildings and, in particular, don't miss the slender tenth-century cross in the churchyard, fourteen feet high and richly carved with pagan and Christian inscriptions.

Kinniside Stone Circle

The Valley of The River Calder

A WEIRD COLLECTION of apparitions in assorted shapes and sizes is glimpsed on the coastal plain as the A595 proceeds from the Gosforth junction north-west. This is no fantasy of the imagination: it is the Sellafield Nuclear Power Station, having changed its name from the original Calder Hall and then Windscale as though to disguise its existence. That the station has nothing to be ashamed of is evidenced by the welcome given to visitors who may visit at almost any time.

Alongside, on the A595, and seemingly undismayed by the monster that has grown up, the inhabitants of the pleasant village of Calder Bridge go about their daily business as if nothing had happened to their environment, discounting threats of radiation and enjoying a peaceful life in the company of the River Calder.

Visitors here in search of natural beauty should turn their backs on Sellafield and head north along a charming side road near the bridge. This road climbs over Cold Fell to Ennerdale Bridge and I have adopted it as the western boundary of the area described in this book: beyond, to the west, are declining foothills and the industrial coastal plain bordering the Irish Sea. The Cold Fell road is an excellent high-level drive for motorists, and offers an easy crossing of the fells for walkers. There is, however, little of immediate interest along the way, except on the descent to Ennerdale Bridge where the Kinniside Stone Circle alongside the road attracts attention: I could never understand why it was not indicated on the maps of the Ordnance Survey, usually so meticulous about antiquities, until reading that it was a fake, put there by a local schoolmaster and his pupils to emulate the works of their ancient forebears.

The River Calder starts its career on the high ridge overlooking Ennerdale and after some early uncertainty elects to flow south where it follows a course roughly parallel to the Cold Fell road. For some miles it is a modest stream not really deserving the status of river and is defined by the slopes of Lank Rigg rising to the east. After an uneventful infancy in wild surroundings, it is first crossed by the primitive arch of Matty Benn's Bridge, a narrow span without parapets across a little gorge. This simple yet picturesque structure (and called Monks Bridge by the Ordnance Survey) is a survivor over many centuries and may be reached from the road at Coldfell Gate by a lane leaving opposite a junction with a road from Egremont.

Matty Benn's Bridge

Below Matty Benn's Bridge the Calder receives its main tributary, Worm Gill, which forms the eastern boundary of Lank Rigg and has a water intake works midway. I have a soft spot for Lank Rigg; it is the most remote of the western fells and getting to it without a car or convenient public transport posed a problem I finally overcame (I forget how) and in celebration of this achievement, which enabled me to complete the compilation of the seventh Pictorial Guide, I left a florin (the old two-shilling coin) under a stone on the summit as a treat for the next person to reach the top and mentioned this benefaction in the book, not expecting that it would ever be found in that isolated spot. But it was: on the day of publication a Whitehaven couple went there and collected the reward. For years after I had reports of others grubbing amongst the summit stones for treasure trove, in vain. Sorry about that!

Now the Calder enters a more fertile landscape with trees, cultivated pastures and a few farms and, within sound of the main road, the venerable and extensive ruins of Calder Abbey appear on the west bank, easily approached from the Cold Fell road. The abbey, dating from the twelfth century, gives far more pleasure to the eyes than anything on offer at Sellafield.

Calder Abbey

Massed conifers in Ennerdale Forest, from Pillar

ENNERDALE

I REMEMBER WALKING along Ennerdale one February morning about fifty years ago. The snows had gone and winter was relaxing its icy grip on a wild landscape that, under a sullen sky, looked aggressively hostile. There was no greenery in the valley, colours were muted, tawny and russet and a drab brown on a patchwork carpet of grasses, sedges and rushes lying battered by storms and awaiting rebirth and regeneration. Wreaths of mist drifted around the high ramparts far above on both sides, revealing momentary glimpses of black and threatening crags before the writhing vapours again hid them from sight. The scene was sombre, the desolation profound. I was alone but did not lack company. A few seabirds hovered overhead happily anticipating better days to come, and the puddles in the rough cart track following heavy rain were alive with colonies of croaking frogs. The stream danced alongside, adding a sparkle of gaiety, the white flashes of cascades lightening the gloom. Yet I lingered often. Ennerdale had an impressive grandeur that day. Beneath the brooding clouds there was a compelling magic in the air that delayed my progress. I have often sensed the presence of fairies in Lakeland but that morning there were only witches.

In those early days, Ennerdale was bare of trees: the harsh and rocky terrain offered them no welcome. But trees were soon to come, a million of them, not born there naturally but brought as foreign prisoners and forced to take root in crowded battalions and live wretched lives deprived of light and air and finally destined to die a brutal death. Ennerdale Valley became Ennerdale Forest, a forest of cripples with withered limbs. The frogs crept away. The songbirds left. The once-colourful tapestries of the fellsides were shrouded in a funeral cloak. Thankfully, the surrounding heights have escaped invasion and desecration by plantations and remain as proud and defiant as ever.

The Black Sail Youth Hostel

Ennerdale is watered by the River Liza, which springs to life in a tumble of boulders below Wind Gap on Great Gable and, being little more than a trickle, is unusually honoured by being named as a river from birth. Through a drop of 1500 feet, the youthful Liza flows down a narrow channel to the valley; there it is strengthened by a tributary, Loft Beck, in an area of drumlins left by a retreating glacier in ages past. A footbridge is reached, carrying a popular path from Black Sail Pass and Wasdale Head, and here Sail Beck scampers down to join in a last taste of freedom before the combined waters are incarcerated and lost to sight within the prison fence of the forest, now directly ahead.

From the footbridge the path goes forward to a humble isolated building, a shepherds' bothy converted to use as a Youth Hostel. With no roads, no traffic and no crowds within many miles, this lonely refuge occupies the most privileged site in Lakeland, a magnificent circle of peaks dictating the itineraries of the fellwalkers who sojourn there.

The Black Sail Youth Hostel stands outside the fringes of the forest, alongside which a path climbs up to Scarth Gap and to Buttermere. The main access to the hostel is provided by a cart track through the forest in the company of the river which is glimpsed momentarily at breaks in the screen of trees.

The memorial bridge over the River Liza

After two monotonous miles, a little clearing offers a respite from the depression induced by the sight of so many crippled conifers and admits to a footbridge over the river, here flowing with the same abandon as on my first visit to Ennerdale but now appearing in a dark avenue that has replaced the flowery banks.

The footbridge was erected by the County Council at the instigation of the Fell and Rock Climbing Club, who shared the cost and adopted it as a memorial to their members who lost their lives in the 1939–1945 war, this being recorded on a block of granite nearby. The bridge, which replaced one fallen into disrepair, was opened at a ceremony in May 1960. It is perhaps the only redeeming feature of the Ennerdale Forest.

The bridge is sited at the foot of a long and steep firebreak in the forest up which a rough path climbs to emerge in open ground below the famous Pillar Rock, which is seen front on with a waterfall coursing down its west side. This awesome tower of naked rock, 600 feet in height, has long been a favourite haunt of cragsmen, who have established a network of climbing routes up its near-vertical faces. Crowning its summit is the High Man, looking down in dismay at the dark skirt of conifers insensitive men have draped along the lower slopes of the mountain he adorns so nobly. Pillar Rock doesn't need fancy trimmings.

High Man on Pillar

The track continues down the valley, still closely confined between plantations except at one point where an open strip of ground on the right carries a rising path to the summit of Red Pike. Further along the track, the High Gillerthwaite Youth Hostel is passed and beyond, at Low Gillerthwaite, the trees relax to permit an open vista across fields to the welcome sight of Ennerdale Water receding into the far distance. Soon a bridge over the river offers an alternative route for travellers who do not have a car awaiting them at the large car park at Bowness Point, a mile further on at the end of the track where, if they decline the help of transport, they can continue on a good path along the north shore of the lake to its feet, passing the site of the ill-fated Anglers Hotel. This was demolished under a threat to raise the water level which then did not happen: the hotel was so near to the edge of the lake that fishing was possible through the windows from comfortable seats in the bar. The path may be continued to a popular camping and picnic area near the outflow.

The alternative path crosses the bridge at Low Gillerthwaite to a path leading along the south shore of the lake: the bridge is the place for farewells to the Liza, here a considerable river after being augmented by several streams plunging down through the forest on the south side of the valley. The walk along the lakeside is easy until confronted by the rocky headland of Anglers Crag, the path rising to pass over the top and descending on the far side; or a rough passage may be forced through the fallen boulders at the base of the crag, one large block having the name of Robin Hood's Chair. On the fellside above are the Crag Fell Pinnacles, a strange group of dissected rock towering about sixty feet in height.

Anglers Crag   *Crag Fell*

Ennerdale Water

Ennerdale's lovely lake has long been a source of contention. For many years, the water authorities have cast envious eyes on this large expanse of fresh water draining from the mountains; indeed, since the last century modest supplies have been abstracted to serve Whitehaven and surrounding areas, but unobtrusively and with little impact on the scenery. But in 1978, the North West Water Authority proposed an ambitious scheme for raising the water level four feet, confining it by lengthy embankments and installing an enlarged weir in order to increase supplies to the nuclear power station at Sellafield and to West Cumbria generally. This proposal, if approved, would have caused serious disruption during construction and permanent disfigurement to the lake and its environs thereafter. It was strenuously opposed by several conservationist and amenity associations teaming together to protect Ennerdale from desecration and preserve the natural beauty of the lake and valley. A spirited campaign was launched to win public support; demonstrations were arranged and posters displayed, a further objection of the protesters being that the valley was within the National Park and entitled by statute to the highest degree of protection. After a Public Inquiry extending over fifty-seven days in 1980, the arguments of the objectors were upheld and their hard work rewarded. Ennerdale and Ennerdale Water were saved.

The outflowing river is the Ehen. It is accompanied to the only village in the valley, Ennerdale Bridge, by a lane leaving a car park near the weir. Beyond, it enters the industrial coastal plain, visiting Cleator and Egremont and then turning with the railway before finally suffering immersion in the sea in the shadow of Sellafield.

A minor road leaves Bowness Point on Ennerdale Water and, joined by another from Ennerdale Bridge, heads north to meet the A5086 on its way from the towns of West Cumbria to Cockermouth. These arteries effectively define the western boundary of the Lake District, having high fells to the east and declining lowlands to the west and in part coinciding with the boundary of the National Park.

Leaving the car park at Bowness Point, a road soon passes the start of the path over Floutern Pass to Buttermere and, a mile further, a short but distinct valley opens on the right. This is Croasdale. However, despite being inside the National Park, I was denied access to the fells here by a farmer who had been let down by walkers breaking his fences and scattering his sheep. Since I think that it is always safer to assume that farmers on their own land are always right, I say no more about it.

Further along the road, before reaching Lamplugh, a path on the right at Felldyke leads into an opening in the fells that is found on investigation to contain Cogra Moss Reservoir. This is an interesting area to explore although new forests restrict progress at the head of the valley. Over the shapely peak of Knock Murton, immediately to the south, are the disused Knockmurton iron ore mines. The former mine road has been adopted as a forest road, and tight fences prohibit access to areas of ground that once provided prolific bilberry harvests. The Forestry Commission have taken advantage of the fact that there are few visitors to this lonely region and have erected a network of fences to ensure that even fewer come in future.

At Lamplugh a road branches to the right for Loweswater, and the A5086 continues directly ahead to Cockermouth with, on its left, the shallow rural valley of the River Marron, traversed in pre-Beeching days by a branch railway of such scenic quality that, had it been preserved would today have been a prime tourist attraction.

A mile out of Cockermouth the road crosses the newly-aligned A66 and descends gently to this interesting old town.

The mouth of a river is usually regarded as the place of debouchure in the sea. Not so at Cockermouth where the mouth of the River Cocker is its meeting with the greater River Derwent. The town has held a market charter since 1221 and there is visual evidence of age in the ruined twelfth-century castle, captured by Robert the Bruce and subsequently subjected to further attacks before being destroyed during the Civil War. Part was later rebuilt and is privately occupied.

Wordsworth's birthplace – by Derry Brabbs and A. Wainwright

Cockermouth

There are other ancient properties and along the wide main street are numerous shops and several hotels, one of which, the Trout, has permanent reminders to its customers that Bing Crosby once stayed there during a fishing holiday. Another notable character associated with the town was Fletcher Christian of *Mutiny on the Bounty* fame; he was born in the nearby village of Eaglesfield. Another earned a statue in the main street, but the most renowned of all Cockermouth's sons was William Wordsworth, born in 1770 in a large house on the main street; this is now owned by the National Trust and is open to the public.

To the modern fraternity of walkers, Cockermouth has an attraction not linked to its history. The town is the gateway to the Buttermere valley, one of the loveliest in creation. And the River Cocker points the way.

THE VALE OF LORTON

To reach the promised land of Buttermere from Cockermouth, the Vale of Lorton must first be traversed, this being a refreshing appetiser for what is to follow. The road into it leaves the suburbs, crosses the new A66 and heads south-east towards a skyline of fells that grows more arresting with every step or turn of the wheels. After a few miles through peaceful countryside, a road junction is reached, the left fork taking advantage of a breach in the bordering fells to ascend the wide valley of Whit Beck and cross Whinlatter Pass to Keswick via Braithwaite.

THE VALLEY OF WHIT BECK

This valley is relatively insignificant and mentioned only because it gives access to a pretty waterfall and the charming village of High Lorton. Two miles further along the road, the B5292, a halt may be made at Scawgill Bridge where there is space for parking. The bridge crosses Whit Beck and a path goes upstream to the pretty waterfall of Spout Force in a gorge. When I first visited, the area around had been newly planted, even choking the path, and only after a grim battle with growing timber was it possible to get a glimpse of the waterfall. I am told the path has now been cleared.

This road is busy in the summer months and unkind to walkers. Those defeated by traffic would do well to turn aside into the sweet village of High Lorton and forget about Spout Force. Set in lovely parkland, with hospitality at the inn, this serene backwater had a famous yew, a veteran under which John Wesley preached.

From the Whinlatter junction, the road to Buttermere continues with the River Cocker in close attendance, passing the few buildings of Low Lorton and entering a wider strath with an exciting skyline high on the left and in the distance ahead. An old highway joins in on the left at Hopebeck: this comes down from Whinlatter Pass when walkers are engaged on the 'Buttermere Round'. A deep cutting splitting the fellside above Hope Farm offers a direct ascent of Hopegill Head, but is an offer open only to hardy pedestrians, the final stages being steep and rough. A mile further along the road, a signpost points the way to Buttermere.

High Lorton

142

Kirkstile church and inn

It needs willpower to ignore any signpost to Buttermere, but here impatience should be curbed by a visit to Loweswater. Go straight ahead past the Scale Hill Hotel, an important staging and stabling post for the Keswick tourists a century ago. Beyond the hotel the road declines to a bridge over the Cocker and then enters the hamlet of Kirkstile which, having a church and an inn, is considered to be the village of Loweswater and is so named on maps.

MOSEDALE

Coming down to Kirkstile from the south is another Mosedale and like the others of that name is dreary and uneventful. The valley is traversed by a path rising out of Kirkstile, following the descending Mosedale Beck and ending in a juicy morass on Floutern Pass. So lacking in incident is this drainage channel that a solitary tree midway is charted on large-scale Ordnance Survey maps and named 'Mosedale Holly Tree'. The first half-mile of the path out of Kirkstile is in popular use for the ascent of Mellbreak which dominates the valley.

I always walked alone on my explorations of the fells, preferring silence to chatter, but one day when passing the Kirkstile Inn I was joined by a foxhound which had been sitting on the doorstep. Together we walked up into Mosedale and there climbed the pathless slopes of Hen Comb to the summit where the dog waited patiently while I made notes and took photographs. Then, without a word being spoken, we returned to the inn where my new friend disappeared inside without even a farewell wave of his tail. Oddly, I missed his quiet company for the rest of the day.

THE LOWESWATER VALLEY

Three lakes lie in a straight furrow through the western fells, seemingly linked as in a chain but their direction of flow does not conform to the same pattern. Buttermere and Crummock Water drain north-west, Buttermere's surplus water entering Crummock Water, the outflow of the latter being the River Cocker. The one out of step is Loweswater, next in line but deflected south-east by slightly higher ground at its western end; it also discharges into the Cocker. In other respects, Loweswater shares the beauty of the others and in the summer months is all the sweeter for being out on a limb, having no commercial distractions and no crowds.

A tree-fringed road runs along the northern shore of the lake, giving retrospective glimpses of the shapely peak of Mellbreak across the placid waters of the lake. The road passes a turn to the isolated community of Mosser and an hotel to reach the pastures around the head of the lake in a district named on maps as Waterend (but which more properly is water's beginning). Here are a few farmsteads known as Places and prefixed by the name of the first settlers (Iredale Place, Hudson Place, Jenkinson Place): a nice way of ensuring immortality.

The road passes out of the valley over an insignificant watershed bound for Lamplugh and the coastal towns. There is a path through the woodlands along the southern shore, this giving access to a pretty waterfall, Holme Force.

Loweswater, cradled in lovely fells, remains as nature intended it to be: a sanctuary of rural peace.

Loweswater

The Buttermere Valley

THE BUTTERMERE VALLEY

FROM THE BUTTERMERE signpost on the Lorton road, a pleasant mile following its direction is a prelude to the wonderful scenery ahead. High on the left are the steep slopes of Whiteside and this is succeeded at Lanthwaite Green by the massive bulk of Grasmoor, at 2791ft the giant of the north-west region. Between the two fells is the deep cutting of Gasgale Gill.

GASGALE GILL

A path from the road leads up to the rocky portals of Gasgale Gill and continues alongside its descending stream, Liza Beck, rising to the high crossing of Coledale Hause over which it may be continued down to Braithwaite. Gasgale Gill is a grim recess overlooked by Gasgale Crags on the flank of Whiteside and the steep scree runs which fall from the lofty skyline of Grasmoor. There is little pleasure to be found here and certainly no tempting location for a picnic.

GRASMOOR LOOKS EVEN more formidable as the road passes Lanthwaite Green, its rugged visage seamed by dark gullies that threaten disaster if approached. But its easy roadside verges offer spaces for parked cars, and as the view forward opens to reveal the High Stile range across Crummock Water, many accept the offer and halt to study the glorious prospect awaiting ahead.

RANNERDALE

The road then descends almost to lake level at the oasis of Rannerdale Farm where green fields are a bright contrast to the dark upthrust of Rannerdale Knotts behind. This peaceful scene has a place in history as the location of a fierce skirmish between the invading Normans and the native English in the years after the Conquest. Our lads won. The pastures are circumvented by paths from the road, and the valley of Rannerdale, coming down the west side of the sharp peak of Whiteless Pike, is entered and continued steeply uphill to higher regions. Rannerdale Beck, in the absence of a path, is a sure guide but a sure guide to trouble, endless scree slopes halting progress. This is a route for masochists only. No sensible walker goes this way twice. The only saving grace is a waterfall in the lower reaches.

THE ROAD ROUNDS a headland, its passage being carved out of rock. Formerly the road climbed over the headland and was then known as Buttermere Hause. The old road is a good springboard for the ascent of Rannerdale Knotts and valley walkers who do not mind a little rough scrambling will be rewarded by magnificent views.

From the headland, still known as Hause Point, the road skirts the base of the Knotts, the open shore of Crummock Water alongside. Soon the head of the lake is reached and the road enters woodlands for the final mile to Buttermere village.

Impatience to get there may be curbed by an inviting path leaving the first cottages on the left. This points the way to the valley of Sail Beck, a happy stream that once operated a mill and now, in retirement, contributes to the joys of the countryside that in scenic quality has no superiors and few equals.

Rannerdale Knotts

Buttermere church

THE VALLEY OF SAIL BECK

The high skyline of fells forming the northern boundary of the Buttermere valley suffers its most pronounced disturbance directly above the village where a vast hollow scooped out of steep slopes carries down the stream of Sail Beck. A good path alongside ascends gently to the rampant bracken, green in summer, russet and gold in winter, to a deeply enclosed watershed, over which it descends with Rigg Beck to Newlands. This a fine crossing, not too strenuous and, for walkers, greatly to be preferred to the road seen climbing to the same destination along the east side of the valley.

THE VILLAGE OF Buttermere, to its credit, has remained as sweet and unspoilt as when I first saw it and, despite an increasing influx of visitors, as charming. Blessed by an idyllic setting in the shelter of majestic fells and graced by mature woodlands, Buttermere is a foretaste of heaven. Some places of endearing memories are humanised and regarded as friends. Buttermere is one such. And its shining jewel is its lovely lake, mirror of an enchanting landscape.

147

Fleetwith Pike across Buttermere

There are two walks that even the most unadventurous of valley ramblers should attempt, each four miles long and having no difficulties. The first, a circuit of the lake, goes along the lane on the left side of the Fish Hotel, one-time home of the legendary Mary of Buttermere, and affords glimpses of the lake backed by Fleetwith Pike before reaching a bridge over the outflow of the lake, Buttermere Dubs. Across the bridge will be seen through the trees the silvery cascades of Sour Milk Gill, falling a thousand feet from an unseen Bleaberry Tarn. The path turns left and skirts the shoreline, and passes through plantations to open ground; here a path rising to the right for Scarth Gap and Ennerdale is ignored and the head of the lake rounded to the road near Gatesgarth Farm. Turn left here until you are again alongside the lake; here a path follows the north shoreline and passes through a rock tunnel and returns to the village, a journey of sustained delight.

The other recommended walk leaves the lane behind the Fish Hotel and crosses a field to Scale Bridge, where a path to the right reaches the south shore of Crummock Water and then rises up an open fellside. It then turns left to a dark and sinister gorge where Scale Force, the highest of Lakeland's waterfalls, plunges 156 feet in graceful leaps from the heights above.

Stronger walkers can continue along the shore of Crummock Water, passing below Mellbreak, to meet the River Cocker as it departs from the lake.

The road from Cockermouth passes below the little church at Buttermere to a junction where a rising strip of tarmac departs for Newlands, the main road continuing up the valley above the lake. A gracious house converted to use as a Youth Hostel is soon passed: this has for many years, through the kindness of the warden, been the base for an annual sponsored walk to benefit my favourite charity, attended by me, not as a participant but as an observer in a comfortable deck chair.

Gatesgarthdale

A short mile further the fellside on the left is split by a great rift choked by boulders, and it was in this fearful ravine one day that I noticed a baby rowan, only a few inches tall, struggling to find a roothold in a crack on the top of a large rock. I mentioned this in the guidebook I was compiling, requesting any subsequent visitors to this grim defile to report on its battle for survival and in the twenty-five years that have passed since then I have had shoals of letters, many photographs and even a poem, from which I have learned of the rowan's steady progress to maturity and that it now bears an annual crop of berries. To my pleasure, I have been told that it is now known as Wainwright's Rowan.

Beyond Gatesgarth Farm, the road is confronted by the soaring upthrust of Fleetwith Pike. A conspicuous white cross on the lower slopes is a memorial to Fanny Mercer, killed in a fall there in 1887. How much nicer to be remembered by a living tree that will carry my name long after I am gone.

GATESGARTHDALE

The road is deflected to the left by the slopes of Fleetwith Pike alongside the descending Gatesgarthdale Beck, crossing it at a bridge to reveal ahead a scene of utter desolation, the ground littered with rocky debris fallen from the ravaged cliffs of Honister Crag high on the right and the disused Yew Crag quarries on the left. The road picks a way through boulders on a final steep climb to the top of Honister Pass, over which it descends to Borrowdale.

WARNSCALE

Travellers on foot bound for Honister have a traffic-free alternative to the hard road in Gatesgarth-dale. By following the intake wall below Fleetwith Pike to the right, an old cart track with remnants of original paving still intact leads up from Warnscale Bottom, deep below the crags of Haystacks, to the open moorland at Dubs Quarry which the track formerly served until closure. A path goes on in the same direction and descends along a derelict tramway to the cutting sheds at Honister.

Nobody says 'Goodbye for ever' to Buttermere. Only 'Au revoir, see you again'.

THE NORTH-WESTERN CORNERSTONE of Lakeland is formed by a compact group of fells not the less attractive for being only of modest elevation: they bid farewell to the River Derwent as it departs from the lakes and mountains to fulfil its destiny in the Solway Firth.

This is an unfrequented area of the National Park, not because of a lack of appeal but because the Forestry Commission have thrown a dark blanket over much of it, denying to walkers their inherited right to wander freely. Here the Commission are firmly established as the greatest of Lakeland's predators, their disfigurement of the landscape greatly exceeding that of the old enemy, Manchester Corporation.

The valleys in the area are little more than minor folds in the hills, the only one effecting a marked penetration of the ground being that of Wythop Beck.

Buttermere from Fleetwith Pike

Skiddaw from the Wythop Valley

THE WYTHOP VALLEY

WYTHOP (PRONOUNCED WITHUP) can be reached along side roads from the A66, arriving at the little community of Wythop Mill where a pleasant tree-fringed lane leads up the valley alongside the descending waters of Wythop Beck. The valley does not conform to pattern and is an oddity: it has no surround of high ground at its head, as have most, but ends in an abrupt declivity at Bassenthwaite Lake. On my first visit, I experienced an amazing illusion at a turn in the lane, where a mighty mountain mass was suddenly revealed some distance ahead. I thought I knew all the Lakeland heights intimately but this I could not recognise. For some moments I stood transfixed, convinced I had discovered something the mapmakers had missed. Then it gradually dawned on me that I was looking at Skiddaw from an unusual angle over the unseen gulf of Bassenthwaite Lake. Silly me!

The Wythop valley is rarely visited yet has many features of interest surviving from the past. Wythop Old Church is on the lower slopes of Sale Fell, on the left, and near the farm of Kelswick are the fragmentary ruins of Wythop's first church, a tablet on an inner wall being inscribed 'SITE OF WYTHOP OLD CHURCH'. This has been replaced by St Margaret's on the road near Wythop Mill, but once a year a public service (necessarily in the open air) is held in the ruins.

Ladies Table was a favourite picnic place for Victorians but is now almost hidden by trees and forgotten. Ladies Table was the name given to a mound with a flat-topped rock apparently so-called as a parody on Lord's Seat nearby; it will be found but not easily on the upper fringes of Wythop Wood.

151

The Silica Brick Works are on the edge of the wood, south of Wythop Hall, and are the substantial foundations of an enterprise that failed. Here in the 1930s buildings were erected, plant installed, a mineral railway line and a new access road made, all to serve the manufacture of silica bricks. The product proved not to be of sufficiently good quality to ensure a profitable return for the outlay. Buildings and plant were dismantled, the workmen dismissed and the site vacated. Today only the road extension to Wythop Hall remains in use.

Wythop Beck and Beck Wythop is a clever distinction of name for two streams that come down side by side from Lord's Seat and is due to their continuance as separate watercourses aiming for different destinations. They part company near Wythop Hall, an insignificant watershed turning them into separate channels. Wythop Beck curves down the valley to Wythop Mill and joins the Derwent; Beck Wythop turns down into Wythop Wood and enters Bassenthwaite Lake.

Wythop Wood covers the fellside above Bassenthwaite Lake for several miles. Long established, it now forms part of Thornthwaite Forest but retains a separate identity by a welcome blend of deciduous and evergreen trees. Hidden from the sight of the busy A66 running along the shore is an administrative centre of the Forestry Commission.

Reached by a rising path from Wythop Cottages on the lakeside is the Alton Memorial, and perched on the edge of a crag in the heart of the forest, with a splendid view of Skiddaw, is a seat constructed of the native green stone with a tablet inscribed 'Thornthwaite Forest. In memory of Wilfred Walton, Head Forester, 1948–1959'. But the most delightful feature of Wythop Wood is the presence of the lovely little roe deer, shyest of creatures. The new plantations to the south are fenced to prevent their intrusion but they have freedom to roam in the old woodlands. The Forestry Commission, so often criticised for insensitivity in their work, deserve commendation for harbouring these gentle animals in their preserves.

Wythop Wood, in short, ends the Wythop valley in a beautiful and interesting flourish.

THE VALLEYS OFF WHINLATTER PASS

THE GROWING VILLAGE of Braithwaite occupies a favoured location in a bay of the Vale of Keswick at the start of a motor road over Whinlatter Pass to Lorton. This popular crossing has gradually become surrounded by dense plantations that conceal the bordering fells and seal off the valleys descending from them. Tortuous forest tracks lead into the jungle from the road and may, if wished, be persisted in through a confusing network to the higher reaches to gain little reward for much doubt and frustration.

GRISEDALE

One of the three Grisedales in the district – the least known and, presumably like the others, the haunt of wild boar or grise – comes steeply down to the road from Grisedale Pike. The open upper reaches, wild and pathless, may be reached after a mile-long battle with young conifers, the only reward for much effort and confusion being the sight of the shapely peak ahead as one emerges from the trees. This should now be regarded as a no-go area for humans and grise.

THE HOBCARTON VALLEY

A few miles further along the road but unsuspected behind a screen of timber, the valley of Hobcarton is similarly afflicted by a choke of conifers, losing for posterity the most impressive sight of Hobcarton Crag at its head. Here too the game is not worth the candle.

COLEDALE

Braithwaite commands the approaches to two other more obvious valleys. One is Newlands, which I have elected to include among the central valleys, and the other is a Braithwaite exclusive, Coledale.

Four miles an hour can be achieved on foot along an excellent wagon-width track that traverses Coledale, straight as a die, to the Force Crag Barytes Mine, with Coledale Beck alongside and Eel Crag a dominant object ahead, almost lost amid heaps of spoil: this an enterprise that has been profitable on and off for many years. The main level carries a danger warning and it should be heeded. The scenery here is dramatic as Low Force tumbles over Force Crag from a higher recess. Below the mine, the beck can be crossed to a rising path to Coledale Hause and the Buttermere valley.

Coledale

PART FOUR

The Northern Valleys

Great Cockup from Longlands
Left Castlerigg stone circle

THE VALE OF KESWICK

THE NORTHERN FELLS form a compact mass of high ground, almost circular in plan and separated from the rest of Lakeland by a wide gap of pastoral land that ensures their complete insularity. This is an area ravaged since the world began by violent natural convulsions. Geologists tell us that even the highest peaks in the group were once under the sea, that the underlying rocks are the oldest in the district, that later and for countless years the land was gripped by a blanket of ice and that only in comparatively recent times, in a period of global warming, the ice cap melted and was carried away by glaciers that scooped out their departing passages like massive bulldozers, leaving behind a sterile landscape littered by debris. In their wake followed channels of melt water which, in the effluxion of time, became rivers charged by nature with the dual mission of draining the fells and fertilizing the vacated hollows, now known as valleys. Their greatest success, under the watchful supervision of Skiddaw, was in transforming a wasteland into a beautiful garden of meadows and woodlands that became known as the Vale of Keswick.

Derwentwater and Keswick

THE RIVER DERWENT flows out of the lake of Derwentwater and, having so far been nurtured and brought up in surroundings of great beauty, now puts his apprenticeship as a creative artist to the test, with Skiddaw as foreman, as many miles of verdant countryside open up ahead. His skills are soon reinforced by those of the River Greta, also experienced in beauty culture, and together they go forward as one under the name of the senior partner, the Derwent. There is a momentary interruption as their waters are crossed by a great new road, the A66 which was the subject of strong opposition by conservationists when first proposed on the grounds that it would permanently scar a lovely landscape and disturb the tranquillity of a peaceful scene. After the event it must be admitted that, despite a constant flow of traffic, the new road has resulted in little disfigurement and disturbance. At one time the river was crossed by a railway, but this, like so many local lines, has fallen silent through premature death.

Contented cows and sheep watch the leisurely flow of the river as it passes between their luxurious pastures, juvenile tributaries join in and attractive farmsteads and small villages are seen at a distance along the base of sheltering fells. Skiddaw nods approval. Life is good in the Vale of Keswick. An opening on the left indicates the Newlands valley, to be described later, and on the right of the A591 a less pronounced cutting above the village of Millbeck promises a mild adventure.

MILL BECK

A ramble upstream from the little settlement of Millbeck on a good path along the west bank promises well but, if enjoyment is the aim, there is little reward in proceeding beyond a weir that releases a waterfall. Above this point, where Skiddaw Little Man is seen as a formidable peak directly ahead, the stream, now known as Slades Beck, comes down a stony defile that may be followed high on the slopes of Skiddaw, but the way is long, the screes relentless and pleasure very elusive.

AFTER SOME MILES of happy unrestrained meanderings along an emerald carpet, the River Derwent enters a less friendly flatland of mosses irrigated by a network of runnels, obviously the flood area of a large expanse of water seen ahead and to which the river, in its role as principal feeder, now directs its flow. Again, as at Derwentwater, it sacrifices freedom in the cause of duty.

This is Bassenthwaite Lake, having the distinction of being the only sheet of water in the district officially recognised as a lake in its name, the others having the suffixes of meres, waters and tarns. Like the hundred other thwaites in Lakeland, the name is shortened to 'thet' in local speech and because Bassenthet is rather a mouthful for everyday use, it is customary to cut it down further simply to Bass. Bassenthwaite, Bassenthet and Bass: all are acceptable.

Both sides of the lake are flanked by dense forests for several miles, rising steeply above important roads: the A66 follows the western shoreline closely and the A591 commences a long and roundabout route from Keswick to Carlisle. This latter road, given more breathing space, is joined at Dancing Gate by the road from Millbeck and then immediately passes below the wooded hill of Dodd, afforested from tip to toe. The barricade of timber relaxes briefly at the hamlet of Little Crosthwaite before resuming as an impenetrable barrier on the right.

The monotony of this part of the journey can be relieved, and should be, by a deviation on the left to the parish church of St Bega.

A lane leads across fields to the shore of the lake and there in complete isolation stands the humble church of St Bega, shy and rather forlorn but immensely proud of its long history and spiritual influence. Dating from the fourteenth century, there is some evidence that it succeeded an earlier church on the same site that may have been founded by St Bega herself. The extreme remoteness of the site, far from habitations and centres of population, lends credence to the belief that it was occupied in prehistoric times as a Druid place of worship. The interior is a simple blend of Norman and Early English architecture, restored in 1874. There are open views across the lake and Skiddaw is a mighty protecting buttress behind.

St Bega's wins affection. Visitors are sorry to leave it to its lonely vigil.

The forest ends abruptly at the Ravenstone Hotel and the road rises gently to a junction at High Side, the A591 descending thence to the foot of the lake, where the Derwent again reasserts a separate identity and, leaving Lakeland behind, soon receives the River Cocker and heads for the sunset and retirement.

The church of St Bega

THE NORTHERN ARC

A T HIGH SIDE a narrow lane goes off to the north, the first link in a chain of quiet roads around the perimeter of the northern fells and from which all forays into their fastnesses must be made. Outside this perimeter, foothills decline west and north to the coastal plain and the Solway Firth, and east to the Pennines. All our interest is centred within, and here we must not expect to find the beautiful lakes and valleys so prevalent in other parts of Lakeland to the south. The northern fells are bare and austere, the valleys sterile. In the interior of an area of almost two hundred square miles there is only one habitation and this is long derelict. But solitude has its favours. There are no gift shops, no timeshares and very little afforestation. And no crowds: in two years of weekend exploration, apart from Skiddaw which has daily visitations, I never met a soul – unless sheep have souls. Nature here is as nature intended it to be, raw, and has never been mollified by human attention. Landscapes are as they have always been ever since the ice went away and glaciers shaped the valleys.

There is little in this area to interest sight-seeing tourists whose activities do not extend beyond simple valley strolls, and only perimeter roads available for the motorists who never stray from their cars.

This will therefore necessarily be a short chapter. High Side is a good starting point for a tour of the northern valleys.

Within a mile after leaving High Side on the A591 north, there is an easing of the steep slopes on the right and an access lane leads up to the farm at Barkbeth. It is set well back and stands guardian over a vast hollow formed by two valleys – Southerndale and Barkbethdale – which come down, with a rising ridge between, from the massive and majestic Skiddaw in the background. These valleys are frequented by sheep and shepherds, rarely by tourists, and in the absence of recognised walkers' paths, they are best left to themselves. In fact, there is little point going further than the farm: I have climbed Skiddaw from both valleys and from the intervening ridge and can recommend all these routes only as a penance for sins.

Continuing along the road, Barkbeth Gill is crossed at Walk Mill Bridge and here receives another Mill Beck coming down from Skiddaw, their combined waters then flowing through Bassenthwaite village to the lake. Mill Beck descends very steeply and although pointing the way to Skiddaw, in no sense can it be considered a valley walk. Passing the farm at Melbecks, a profound hollow opens up on the right. This is very definitely a valley, bringing down a considerable stream, Dash Beck. It is traversed by a rough road that can be followed without fear of trespass.

THE DASH VALLEY

From the road opposite Peter House, a lane enters the valley, serving as access to Dash Farm on the far bank of the stream, but before arriving at the crossing, a branch to the right turns off and continues up the valley. This is the supply road to the isolated Skiddaw House, still some miles ahead, and offers a splendid walk, with no fear of going astray, into the open wilderness of Skiddaw Forest.

Leaving the Dash Farm access, the narrow road passes below the shattered cliffs of Dead Crags, and down a grassy slope on the left can be seen Dash Falls, also known as Whitewater Dash, leaping in cascades to lower levels.

The road to Skiddaw House curves round to the top of Dash Fells, crossing the stream at a packhorse bridge to the far bank, along which it continues for two further miles. Skiddaw's north ridge rises even higher on the right, with the heather slopes of Great Calva on the left. Ahead is a widening landscape of a vast wilderness gripped by an awesome stillness, a desolate wasteland frozen into silence and loneliness absolute. There is a strange beauty in the scene, too, recognised only by those who prefer solitude. Skiddaw Forest is a forest without trees except for a small plantation that comes into sight on the approach and marks the location of Skiddaw House. The presence of old shooting butts in the vicinity suggests that the building may originally have been a hunting lodge, but within a long memory it was occupied five days a week by shepherds, becoming abandoned about twenty years ago when the last resident retired for a life without sheep. The house commands a long view down the valley of the River Caldew. A path continues south to Threlkeld or Keswick, offering a fine expedition on foot through the northern fells, solitary but safe.

Dash Falls

159

THE ROAD GOES on beyond Peter House and arrives at Cassbeck Bridge where Dash Beck crosses to more verdant surroundings alongside a side road to Bassenthwaite village. Rising on the right now are the Uldale Fells, a close-knit group of moderate height intersected by streams: it is an area that strangers should explore only if accustomed to rough walking and armed with a large-scale map. Here, in harsh terrain, there are no pretty dells and picnic places; few other walkers will be met, and little hope of rescue if lost or injured. I spent several visits unravelling the intricacies of the Uldale Fells, feeling that I was the only man on earth and enjoying every minute.

The road next enters the little settlement of Orthwaite, a pleasant oasis with an attractive Hall. From here a walk may be made that introduces the Uldale Fells, links three valleys by paths that in places involve passing over rough ground but with little climbing and ends at my favourite spot in the area, Trusmadoor.

Above *Orthwaite Hall*   Below *View from Orthwaite*

160

TRUSMADOOR

A farm track, accompanied by a wall, leaves Orthwaite heading south-east, below the rising slopes of Little Cockup, and when abreast of Brocklecrag Farm, a path turns left to pass below the crag that gave its name to the farm. From there is a fine prospect over the Dash valley below. The path follows another wall, and when this turns away goes on, crosses an old bridleway and veers north into Burntod Gill, more a ravine than a valley. The path becomes sketchy as it persists along the side of Great Cockup but correct identification is confirmed by the dome of Meal Fell directly ahead. Upon reaching the base of this fell, the stream changes direction and comes down from the right under the name of Frozen Fell Gill. At the bend the path turns sharp left and enters Trusmadoor.

Trusmadoor has the appearance of a ready-made railway cutting and is usually occupied and enjoyed by grazing sheep. Although conforming to the pattern of a valley, it does not carry a stream and is more usually considered a pass, as the name implies. The path through Trusmadoor continues north to cross the head waters of the River Ellen and rejoin the road at Longlands, thus ending a circular tour of introduction to the Uldale Fells with Trusmadoor the solitary highlight.

Trusmadoor

STOCKDALE

The road beyond Orthwaite permits glimpses of a large expanse of water on the left: this has the name of Over Water, the only lake in the northern arc of Lakeland. As Great Cockup declines on the right, the landscape opens up and when a road branches off to the village of Uldale, an access road opposite leads into the valley of Stockdale.

Stockdale's main contribution to the geography of Lakeland is as the source of the River Ellen, a major watercourse which leaves the valley to weave a way through the towns and villages of the coastal plain to discharge into the Solway Firth at Maryport. There is no recognised walkers' path beyond Stockdale Farm and little inducement to proceed into the marshy hinterland of the river's gathering grounds, although there the path between Longlands and Trusmadoor may be joined to give an alternative way back to the road.

161

THE ROAD NEXT arrives at the farming complex of Longlands. Here a stream comes down from the south-east, marking the boundary of Longlands Fell. It is accompanied by the path from Trusmadoor, but has nothing of immediate interest other than a sheepfold and dipping pens. This watercourse is an example of the many in the northern fells that do not occupy well-defined valleys: some tumble from the heights over grass slopes and make no impact on the ground or the landscape which serve merely as gutters. I am not skimping my brief in omitting detailed reference to such, having traced them all to their sources or surveyed them from a distance without finding any features deserving of special mention. My narrative is designed for valley ramblers and is therefore confined to the wide hollows carved by glaciers and since matured by the ministrations of nature into pleasant straths rewarding a visit. The northern fells offer exhilarating exercise for the seasoned fellwalker, with no hindrances or fences, large conifer plantations or no-go areas, but the more sedate valley stroller is less well catered for, and even in the simplest of perambulations boots must be the order of the day: there is no place here for sandals and shops.

At Longlands the road may be left in favour of an old highway that skirts the lower slopes of Longlands Fell, more intimately trending eastwards to cross another watercourse, Charleton Gill. Before reaching the stream, a bridleway strikes off to the right and in five minutes comes alongside where a descending tongue of land narrows to a delicate knife-edge arete, a feature that so impressed the Ordnance surveyors that they gave it the name of Saddleback. The bridleway continues uphill to the central heights of the area but is for fellwalkers and horses only.

Charleton Gill

Mine adit at Dale Beck

ROUGHTON GILL

The old road goes on along the base of Brae Fell to Greenhead, there joining a road which continues eastwards to the little settlements of Branthwaite and Fell Side. On this section of the journey, there is awareness of an opening in the barrier of fells on the right, obviously a valley of large dimensions penetrating deep into the high ground beyond and inviting inspection. This is Roughton Gill, pronounced Rowt'n Gill.

Whatever one's definition of a valley may be, there is no doubt that Roughton Gill qualifies. There is ease of approach and access to the lower reaches where surviving features of industrial decay are an added interest. This is the site of the once renowned and long abandoned Roughtongill Lead Mines.

The simplest way of entering the valley is along the old mine road from Fell Side. This is the site of a smelt mill, of which only the foundations remain, succeeded by spoil heaps, and eager explorers will find the cave entrances of mine levels nearby. The descending stream, Dale Beck, is joined by tributaries, Ramps Gill and Birk Gill, as the walk continues up the valley but easy progress ends on reaching steeper ground where the beck rushes down in a series of cascades, with the adit of a mine level at the foot of the falls.

Above the cascades, the beck points the way over rising and rougher ground to the central heights of the area, Little Sca Fell and Great Sca Fell, both having altitudes in excess of 2000ft but not comparing in severity with their worthier namesake in the south of Lakeland.

Roughton Gill is the graveyard of a failed enterprise and like all other places of death once vibrant with activity, there is an air of sadness beneath the shroud of silence. Perhaps Dale Beck's cascades are only falling tears.

Caldbeck church and, right, *the grave of John Peel*

PLACES OF REFRESHMENT are few and far between in the northern fells, and weary travellers at Fell Side will probably gravitate to the attractive village of Caldbeck, two miles down the road, which has resources to meet most needs of the flesh and has, as added bonuses, the gravestone of the famous John Peel in the churchyard and a mediaeval Priest's Mill with waterwheel, restored and converted to use as a mining museum.

High Pike, rising to 2157 feet south of the village is pierced with the scars of extensive mining operations on the higher slopes. Three mines, now defunct, were centred in a labyrinth of levels and shafts, fenced since abandonment, and an aerial ropeway carried ore down from the Potts Gill Mine to the valley at the hamlet of Nether Row, reached by road from Caldbeck.

I spent much time in the area of the mines, compiling a map pinpointing the many features of interest and found the task a most fascinating exercise. But as the Potts Gill Mine and the other two, Sandbed Mine and Driggeth Mine, are all above the 1400ft contour, they are outside the scope of this book, although determined pedestrians without the expenditure of too much effort may reach the mining area by following Potts Gill upstream from Nether Row. There is, however, an easier access from the east, along the valley of Carrock Beck. To get there the eastern shoulder of High Pike, oddly named West Fell, must be rounded and a visit made by road from Caldbeck to the village of Hesket Newmarket.

The villagers of the ancient settlement of Hesket Newmarket are housed in cottages ranged along both sides of a wide green that adds spaciousness to a peaceful scene enhanced by the wooded banks of the River Caldew. A country road leaves here and heads due south, ultimately reaching the A66 after defining most effectively the eastern boundary of the northern fells: on the right throughout is a succession of steep slopes broken by three pronounced valleys, and on the left undulating farmlands extend to the River Eden and are backed in the far distance by the Pennines. Lakeland ends abruptly along this road.

164

Hesket Newmarket

After two miles, the road reaches the farm of Calebrack where a mine road punctuated by adjacent levels and shafts climbs over West Fell to the High Pike mines, but an easier approach is available by continuing a further half-mile along the road to where the fellside recedes to give a view along a wide opening watered by Carrock Beck.

THE VALLEY OF CARROCK BECK

Before reaching the bridge over Carrock Beck, a mine road turns up the valley and gives easy access on foot alongside the stream, which higher changes its name to Drygill Beck as the gradient steepens on a final rise to the Driggith Mine. The Sandbed Mine is a short walk further over an area pierced by shafts which, although fenced, need care in exploration. Return to the road the same way.

THE ROAD GOES on, unenclosed, along the base of Carrock Fell but distanced from its lower slopes by a remarkable desert of boulders, among which are deserted mines, quarries and, it is thought, traces of prehistoric settlements. On the roadside fringe of this extraordinary wasteland of littered rocks is a farm with the appropriate name of Stone Ends. Nearby is a tight concentration of boulders known as the Apronful of Stones.

Travellers along the road, on foot or on wheels, will have no appreciation of the unique features that combine to make Carrock Fell one of the most interesting of Lakeland heights. The cliffs are composed of gabbro, unusual in the district; the summit is ringed by the decaying walls of an ancient British fort, and at the far end of a plateau of scattered rocks and heather is the famous Carrock Mine where rich veins of metals and minerals have been worked over many years. Carrock is a special fell, revealing its secrets only to those who climb out of the valleys.

MOSEDALE

After passing Stone Ends, the road passes through a little colony of buildings at the entrance to a long side valley. This is the last of the many Mosedales in Lakeland and the only one giving its name to a village at its entrance. It is further distinguished by carrying the largest stream in the northern fells, and having a good tarred road inland for two miles. Not long ago a report of lions in the valley gave it greater distinction, these animals being kept in captivity at a large estate there.

A road leaves Mosedale village and runs along the north bank of the Caldew below the interminable scree slopes of Carrock Fell, passing the estate of Welbank. The road arrives at a bridge over Grainsgill Beck, which comes down on the right from the Carrock Mine, most renowned for rich supplies of wolfram. When I was there thirty years ago, the mining operations had ended and the area was a shambles of ruined huts and collapsing cottages; the ground was pockmarked with levels and shafts and heaps of spoil, a tremendous cutting had been carved out of the side of Coomb Height and the one bright spot in a depressing scene was a slender waterfall in a tributary, Brandy Gill. Since that early visit, the mine has been reopened and worked, adding a new peril of forcible expulsion for amateur explorers trespassing on the site.

In the river bed nearby appears one of nature's little aberrations: an intrusion of granite in an area composed predominantly of slates and shales.

From the bridge, a path continues up the valley on the north bank of the river for four further miles with little incident or excitement, aiming directly for the huge mass of Skiddaw ahead. Here in the heart of Skiddaw Forest solitude is supreme. Occasional sheepfolds are passed and it will be noted that they are circular in shape, as in Scotland, and not rectangular as is common in Lakeland. Eventually, after a long hour of easy walking, the path crosses the river at a footbridge and soon comes to a full stop at Skiddaw House, standing in lonely isolation at the head of the valley.

Mosedale

Mosedale's greatest attraction, once fashionable with Victorian sightseers, is Bowscale Tarn which occupies a glacial hollow in the side of Bowscale Fell on the south flank of the valley. It is reached by a rising path from the road at Bowscale, a little further on from Mosedale village. The path there involves a thousand feet of climbing but it is well graded, giving excellent aerial views of the valley, and ends with dramatic effect as the tarn is suddenly revealed in a surround of shadowy crags. There is a legend of two undying fish in the tarn, mentioned in a poem by Wordsworth. Contrary to the opinions of other writers, Bowscale Tarn gets my vote as the finest tarn in Lakeland.

Mungrisdale

MUNGRISDALE

The road leaves Bowscale and curves round the base of a steep fellside, passing the little church of St Kentigern, and reaches the small village of Mungrisdale within a mile. At this pleasant backwater, which has the luxury of an inn, the River Glenderamackin is crossed at a sharp bend and is seen to come down a short valley on the right.

The valley of Mungrisdale, its name suggesting that wild boar once roamed here, is traversed by a rough lane to a waterworks building and also by a path alongside the descending river. Almost at once Bullfell Beck comes round a tongue of land from Bowscale to join the river, which now changes direction, rounding the base of Souther Fell and emerging from a more pronounced opening southwards, a path following closely.

BANNERDALE

A new vista is now revealed, the long cliffs of Bannerdale Crags forming a high skyline on the right, the steep slopes of Souther Fell crowding in on the left. Half a mile on, Bannerdale Beck descends from a wild hollow beneath Bannerdale Crags. Bannerdale's name implies a valley not justified by the shallow channel down which it pours, nor is the hollow marking its place of baptism deserving of the status of a valley, being more like a cwm or cove. However, the crags form an impressive surround.

The main valley goes on to another bend and here, at a footbridge, the A66 is only half a mile away over the low ridge to the south. The river and path continue, bringing Blencathra into intimate view, but progress behind the footbridge is not advised if a return is to be made to the village.

The River Glenderamackin pursues a most erratic course through folds in the fells and seemingly in all directions. At Mungrisdale village, it departs from its confines and turns south into a pastoral environment and enjoys a more leisurely pace amid scenes no longer hostile and lonely, but friendly.

The road, now in its final stages, leaves Mungrisdale and makes a beeline through an open countryside to join the A66 and its unceasing stream of traffic. The quiet life is over. We are back in tourist Lakeland. And ahead in the far distance is the serrated skyline of the central fells, promising a wonderland of beauty and adventure, and we hasten there, like exiles coming home, with the River Greta as our guide.

Derwentfolds

THE VALLEY OF THE RIVER GRETA

AFTER PASSING under the A66, the Glenderamackin is joined by Trout Beck, draining a wide moorland to the south, and their combined waters descend in looping curves to a wide and fertile valley where they become known as the River Greta. The A66, recently re-aligned, heads more directly for the valley's capital, Threlkeld. On this section of the journey, the road and river, and the track of a disused and dismantled railway, pass below the furrowed visage of Blencathra which displays a savage ferocity without parallel in the district. Abrupt buttresses leaping up to the sky are pierced by a succession of ravines choked with boulders which, although bringing down streams and therefore technically valleys, must be regarded as severely out of bounds for average walkers and have no place in this book. In other respects, the valley of the Greta repays exploration. Men were settled here long before the dawn of history, as is testified by the decaying walls of an ancient village on the lower slopes of Threlkeld Common, and for centuries the roots of Blencathra were plundered for their mineral wealth.

Threlkeld, once a mining village, retains some old interests. Here are the kennels of the Blencathra Foxhounds and a body of supporters and followers. Old traditions are maintained. Some amenities have gone; the railway station is no more and a long-established sanatorium is now a holiday centre. Tourism is the new industry and camping and caravan sites are sprouting in the vicinity. A quiet no-through-road leaves the village and rises along the side of Blease Fell to the site of the former sanatorium, gloriously located high above the valley with a commanding view over central Lakeland. I used to envy the people who were ill in this delectable spot, but conversion to a holiday centre put a stop to such wishful thinking. Lakeland is for individuals, preferably travelling alone not in the company of guided parties. There was a bus service to the sanatorium, but no longer. The road ends in a path that turns a corner into the valley of the River Glenderaterra.

Castlerigg Stone Circle

THE GLENDERATERRA VALLEY

THE ROAD FROM Threlkeld to the former sanatorium, now Blencathra Centre, gives the easiest access to the valley of the River Glenderaterra which provides excellent and easy walking. At the end of the tarred road, a path continues rounding a corner of Blease Fell and then heading due north with the river below on the left. At this point, relics of an old lead mine may be seen, and just here a tributary is crossed, on slabs: this is Roughton Gill coming down from Blencathra. After another half-mile, another tributary is crossed, Sinen Gill, which is remarkable for an upstream of granite blocks, aliens in this lane of slates and shales. The path now crosses to the west bank alongside a wall and there joins a path from Keswick, this offering an alternative route of return via Gale Road and Applethwaite. But if a better defined objective is sought, it will be found by a further half-hour's walking to where an oasis of trees indicates the location of Skiddaw House. But, to end a fine walk with a damp squib, no form of refreshment will be found there.

The five miles from Threlkeld to Keswick complete this tour of the perimeter of the northern fells. The River Greta, shyer and much less obtrusive in the landscape, receives the Glenderaterra at a hidden rendezvous and follows a parallel course along the base of the wooded slopes of Latrigg. The A66, realigned to avoid the congested streets of Keswick, cuts a swathe through the woods, sharing with the river a delightful finale to the tour. The River Greta joins the Derwent and the A66 enters the Vale of Keswick.

One deviation in this last section is compulsory. On the brow of the hill to the south, and reached along a signposted byroad, is the Castlerigg Stone Circle, a great ring of boulders occupying an open site with an unrivalled prospect of the surrounding fells. This remarkable shrine is best appreciated when the visiting crowds have departed at the end of the day.

PART FIVE

The Central Valleys

Wetherlam from Little Langdale
Left *Lower Borrowdale from King's How*

THE THIRLMERE VALLEY

VISITORS BOUND FOR Keswick and northern Lakeland from the south usually arrive along the main road artery through the district, the A591 (unless driving heavy vehicles which are banned on this route). After enjoying an interlude of beautiful scenery as they traverse the Rothay valley, they reach the highest point on the journey on Dunmail Raise, following a steep climb from Grasmere. Here a new and more saturnine prospect opens up ahead, the sunny open pastures of the Rothay being succeeded by a long defile darkened by extensive plantations on the enclosing slopes, with a long serpentine stretch of water occupying the floor of the valley and the mighty mass of Helvellyn presiding over all and the distant northern fells closing the horizon.

The water in view is Thirlmere, Manchester's first reservoir in Lakeland. In the later years of the nineteenth century, that city's growing demand for additional water supplies led to a survey of the district by their engineers, travelling on horseback, in a search for a potential provider of new sources. In the event, this valley was chosen for the development of a major reservoir to be known as Thirlmere and rights were acquired by Royal Assent for operations to proceed. Hitherto there were two small natural lakes in the valley with a footbridge passing between them to link the eastern shore with the little colony of Armboth on the west side, but Armboth vanished beneath the oncoming flood, only retaining its name on ancient signposts a hundred years later.

Outraged, Helvellyn watched as armies of workers tore up the footstool gardens he had created along the valley and nurtured with his streams through the ages, and frowned as they cleared a three-mile trench to contain a water level soon to be raised by 54 feet and in which he would forever have to bathe his roots. There were many public protests against this rape of a lovely part of Lakeland and Helvellyn had to accept his new trimmings.

Operations continued over a decade: the groundwork of the reservoir was prepared with containing walls, new roads and plantations of conifers designed to hold back rainfall in times of drought. In 1890, the dam was completed and a slow transformation took place as the fifty streams contributing to the valley could find no escape and infilled. Some method had to be devised for conveying the augmented supplies of water to Manchester and this was achieved by boring a 96-mile aqueduct through the crusts of Westmorland and Lancashire with draw-off points to serve other communities along the way in times of need. The whole length was cleverly contrived so that the water flowed by gravity without recourse to pumping.

Manchester Corporation and the Forestry Commission have been the greatest predators in Lakeland over the past century. They were not welcome intruders, both being strongly opposed by conservationists and lovers of the district. They have done much to destroy the original character of the scenery and done little to enhance its natural charm. Enough has been more than enough. But it must be conceded that a hundred years of maturity have added a new attractiveness to the Thirlmere valley, best appreciated when viewed from a distance. In the case of Thirlmere, all is forgiven.

The A591 declines sharply north from Dunmail Raise to the head of the reservoir, passing on the way an inscribed tablet set in the lower end of the roadside wall on the right. The Lake District is well endowed with memorial stones and cairns: some commemorate the achievements of local worthies, others are reminders of historic incidents, many more mark the sites of tragic accidents, and a few immortalise favourite foxhounds. This one on the side of the A591 pays a touching tribute to a horse that served his master faithfully for many years 'and whose only fault was dying'. Speeding motorists pass this without noticing it but from me, long aware of its message, it never fails to jerk a tear.

172

Thirlmere Valley from Steel Fell

Further down the road, a branch still signposted Armboth turns away to the left and the narrative will return to this point after first continuing the journey along the main road. In a short distance, the site of the vanished hamlet of Wythburn, pronounced Wyburn, is reached. Within easy memory there was an inn here, a terrace of cottages and a church. Only the humble church has survived the traumatic happenings in the valley, although a recent innovation is a car park to accommodate the vehicles of the many walkers who use Wythburn as a popular springboard for the ascent of Helvellyn.

Soon the road comes abreast of Thirlmere, permitting occasional glimpses of its waters through a screen of bordering trees which contains and conceals the administrative buildings of the reservoir. An open break in the plantations on the right gives a very steep access to the old lead mines of Helvellyn and may be continued with much effort to the summit.

Then the road enters a long claustrophic avenue bordered by mature trees on both sides, and midway, on a high bank over the roadside fence, is the Rock of Names retrieved from the former shore road before the floods came and removed to its new site when the present road was made at a higher level. This rock, a boulder bearing the inscribed names of Wordsworth and many of his contemporaries, is difficult to find and because of damage difficult to identify. After more miles robbed of views by trees, the road suddenly emerges as from a tunnel into open country with a view forward to Blencathra. At the exit from the trees, another well-patronised car park has been provided and to appease criticisms that their tight plantings have created a closed shop excluding walkers, the authorities have now opened some forest paths to the public.

The A591 next descends to Thirlspot where, behind the large hostelry of the King's Head, a ladder of white-washed boulders climbs the fellside on the long White Stones path back to Helvellyn. Beyond the hotel in a pleasant environment are the spaced cottages of Fisher Place, a workers' community in a location known as Dale Head. This seems to be rather curiously named because the area seems better described as the foot of the Thirlmere valley, but justified on the site by the appearance, directly ahead and leading off the A591, of a green strath pointing the way to Blencathra with a beckoning invitation hard to resist. This is St John's in the Vale, too good to miss, and the narrative will return to it shortly. The main road, now a broad highway, reaches the scattered hamlet of Legburthwaite and here forks. This junction will be rejoined after a description of an alternative route down the Thirlmere valley with more to commend it than the A591 and for this the narrative must return to the Armboth signpost at the head of the reservoir since this gives direction to a quieter road alongside Thirlmere and, if time is not of the essence, greatly to be preferred.

THE WYTHBURN VALLEY

The alternative road departs from the A591 and curves west around the headwaters of the reservoir, soon crossing its main feeder, Wythburn Beck, here seen descending a rough defile on the left.

Wythburn Beck has its source high in the fells around Greenup Edge and the valley it has carved offers a backdoor route to the Langdale Pikes, but not without reservations: in the upper reaches there is an extensive swamp, prominently named by the Ordnance Survey, and with evident relish, as The Bog. The beck, after passing under the road, courses towards the vanished hamlet of Wythburn and it is likely that the valley hereabouts was known as Wythburn before Manchester came along and adopted the newly invented name of Thirlmere.

Launchy Gill

THE ROAD CLOSELY follows the western shore of the reservoir all the way to the dam and is scenically rewarding except when edged by an ugly tidemark in times of drought. The majestic pile of Helvellyn is seen throughout across the water, and little bays and headlands add an intimate interest to the journey. Shortly after Wythburn, a path leaves the road at Dob Gill for Harrop Tarn and a high crossing to Watendlath. Then the bordering slopes are crowded with plantations, punctuated by streamlets descending from the heights of Armboth Fell above. The greatest incision in the fellside is formed by Launchy Gill in a hurried tumble of cataracts and waterfalls; where a rough scramble upstream, not kindly disposed to wearers of inadequate footwear, soon brings into view on the south bank a huge boulder, fallen from the cliffs above and come to rest on a slender keel. It is a boulder so big that it has not been allowed to remain anonymous; it is named the Tottling Stone.

174

Helvellyn across Thirlmere

Elsewhere in the gloom and silence of the Thirlmere forests are decaying evidences of the community life that existed here before Manchester came to end it: ruined farmsteads, shepherds' huts, overgrown cart tracks, crumbling allotment walls green with mould and moss, even a whisky still and a cockpit, all fading into a forgotten history buried under a dark shroud of growing timber.

As the environs of the ill-fated settlement of Armboth are approached, the adjoining fellside relaxes its steepness and an open break in the trees allows the passage of a path from the road rising at an easy gradient to cross the ridge and descend to Watendlath.

The plantations return for the last mile to the dam and the fretted shoreline affords retrospective views of the full length of Thirlmere backed by Helvellyn and, to be fair to Manchester, it must be conceded that the early criticisms and opposition to their coming has not been justified by subsequent events. The area has matured into an impressive beauty.

The road crosses the dam under the towering ramparts of Raven Crag, and with the stream released therefrom in close attendance, rejoins the A591 at Smaithwaite Bridge half a mile beyond the Legburthwaite road junction.

The last few miles of the A591 to Keswick are laid across an open and undulating countryside, not following a valley system, but midway a hidden glen on the left is passed unnoticed. This is Shoulthwaite.

175

Grisedale Pike

THE SHOULTHWAITE GLEN

The Shoulthwaite valley is more readily identifiable when travelling in the reverse direction from Keswick, when the vertical profile of Iron Crag, seen starkly against the sky, marks its location. The valley descends untidily between Raven Crag and High Seat and has little to inspire a visit although the curious may go in search of Litt's Memorial which is fast becoming unrecognisable and difficult to decipher on the flanks of the latter fell.

As the last rise of the A591 is topped before the long descent into Keswick, there is presented to travellers the crowning bonus of the journey: a prospect of surpassing magnificence best seen from the adjoining roadside field. This is a grand view of Borrowdale and Derwentwater below, Bassenthwaite Lake in the distance across the verdant Vale of Keswick and a wonderful array of peaks under the surveillance of old Skiddaw. It all seems too good to be true, much more rewarding than we poor mortals deserve. No wonder Lakeland keeps calling us back.

THE VALE OF ST JOHN

BACK AT THE Legburthwaite road junction, the unceasing swirl of traffic on the A591 may be departed from by following the right fork towards the steep-sided valley now directly ahead, variously known as St John's Vale, The Vale of St John and St John's in the Vale. The noise of cars diminishes and is soon lost as progress is made along this quiet byway.

Seen overtopping the trees on the right is the huge buttress of Castle Rock, promising high adventure for expert rock-climbers and a threat of danger to others who venture upon it.

Accompanying the road is St John's Beck freshly released from Thirlmere, and after receiving Mill Gill from Great Dodd above on the right, both beck and road enter the jaws of the valley to enjoy an all-pervading peace that contributes so much to its rustic charm. The road winds through emerald pastures and copses of trees with the beck an ever-present joy; sheep graze happily and undisturbed, and the intervention of man in the rural scenery is restricted to a few neat farmsteads and allotment walls. Everything in the valley breathes contentment.

After two fragrant miles, the fellside of Clough Head on the right steepens into craggy outcrops and Sandbed Gill comes down to the road as a petrified torrent of stones. Next is a succession of abandoned quarries, and at Wanthwaite an old cart track takes off to cross the northern slopes of Clough Head bound for Dockray and Ullswater: an easy and enjoyable expedition on foot. With the huge bulk of Blencathra now filling the view ahead, the road reaches Threlkeld and the A66, and the beck joins the River Greta; this brings to an end a sweet valley that makes friends on first sight and admirers for life.

The main centre of attraction in the valley and almost a place of pilgrimage for countless visitors is the venerable old church of St John's. This is situated on a low ridge on the west side and is reached from the road by a lane in harmony with a lovely setting, its mellowed stones offering an escape for quiet meditation and thanksgiving for the wondrous beauty all around.

The Vale of St John

GREAT LANGDALE

GREAT LANGDALE SHARES with the Rothay valley and Borrowdale the distinction of being one of the most tourist-populated valleys in Lakeland. But perhaps the word distinction, which implies pride of achievement, is not appropriate to the changed circumstances in these valleys since the turn of the century. When Nature completed her masterly landscape architecture ages ago and later the early dalesmen smoothed the rough places and furbished them with rich pastures and woodlands, then indeed there was distinction, rare and flawless, in the scenery thus created. Time was, within living memory, that a walker could wander all day in Langdale and enjoy undisturbed peace with the songs of birds and the murmur of waters as a musical accompaniment; he would meet only a few others, and they of like mind, intent on quiet appreciation of the wonderful surroundings. We walked in fairyland. A solitary bus took us into the valley from Ambleside in the mornings and came back for us in the evenings. Those were halcyon days, gone, never to return.

After the war, men's further contribution to this and other valleys has been to add blemishes where once there was perfection. The increasing invasion of motor cars and coaches, insensitively urged to visit the district by tourist boards and local authorities whose primary responsibility is to preserve the sanctity of their unique natural heritage, has led to the felling of trees and clearance of land to provide parking spaces; and sheep have been outlawed from their grazing grounds which are now used as camping and caravan sites. Inevitably commercial enterprises have sprung up like mushrooms to cater for the demands of noisy crowds of visitors, many of whom show little respect for the glories around them and prefer transistor radios to the muted sounds of a rural countryside. Local traffic is of course acceptable as part of the life of the community, but the mighty leviathans on wheels that choke the narrow roads are unwelcome and should be exiled. Langdale, which we old-timers knew and revered as a secret paradise, is becoming a free-for-all.

Yet these latterday disfigurements and irritations are merely pinpricks in the vast canvas the valley presents to its visitors. Great Langdale it is and great it will always be. The guardians of the valley are the Langdale Pikes, ranged like crouching lions eternally watching the happenings far below, often frowning at what they see but generally of benign disposition. They offer a welcome to those who come as on a pilgrimage to pay homage at the thrones of the gods and even enjoy a friendly tussle with the more active who climb up to pull the hairs on their chests. And they are part only of a majestic surround of peaks that cradle the valley in a loving embrace. Despite my moanings about the rape of beautiful scenery, I would never seek to keep appreciative admirers of natural grandeur out of Langdale; indeed, I would recommend all such to visit it and enjoy a visual feast. My regret is that they will not see it, pristine and unspoiled, as I first saw it sixty years ago.

The road into Langdale leaves the A591 at Waterhead and skirts the shore of Windermere and the site of the Roman fort of *Galava* to reach Rothay Bridge, where it is joined by another from Ambleside. Over the bridge, the base of Loughrigg Fell is rounded, passing the unseen confluence of Langdale's river, the Brathay, with the Rothay on the last stage of their entry into Windermere. At the neat and attractive cottages of Clappersgate, a side turning leads to Hawkshead. The road continues west, passing below the gardens of White Craggs and enters a shady avenue of mature trees screening the Brathay on the left and giving access over a bridge to Brathay church. Then the road goes round an open field containing a swelling of the river into a small tarn known as Skelwith Pool. Then around a bend, where a minor road shoots off to Grasmere, it heads directly for an interesting complex of buildings at Skelwith Bridge.

Near Skelwith Bridge

Most visitors to Langdale halt at Skelwith Bridge where the hotel and a terrace of workers' cottages have been augmented by a large café, tea-rooms, a showplace of local crafts and a gift shop: innovations to quench the thirst of tourists. This thriving little community on the wooded banks of the Brathay stands at a crossroads, the A593 here departing for Coniston and a minor road crossing a ridge to Grasmere, each revealing scenic delights. But the finest natural attraction hereabouts is provided a little further along the Langdale road where there is access to the accompanying river. An abandoned mill race can be crossed to the Brathay's only fit of temper, its waters plunging furiously down a constricted rocky channel. This is Skelwith Force.

Beyond the Force, the road soon emerges from its bordering trees and reaches the open expanse of Elterwater Common; here there is an uninterrupted view of the head of the valley presided over by the Langdale Pikes: an exciting prospect that beckons irresistibly. But first a short detour should be made to Elterwater village nearby on the left, backed by the heathery heights of Lingmoor Fell. Here Great Langdale Beck empties into the small attractive lake of Elterwater, as does the River Brathay, flowing round the fell from the unseen valley of Little Langdale. And from the exit of the lake the Pikes again exert their dominance in the scene, as they do wherever they appear in a view.

The Langdale Pikes

Elterwater village has the appearance of a long-settled rural community, isolated from the few other centres of population in Langdale yet occupying a privileged location on the edge of open country and having the lovely lake that shares its name. The origins of the village are related to industry: farming, quarrying and gunpowder manufacture were basic to the local economy in former years, the workers being housed in terraces of small cottages and provided with an inn and a shop. Times have changed. Farming and quarrying remain active but the derelict site of the gunpowder works has been taken over by the major new industry of tourism and is now a time-share development.

Here as elsewhere in the district, the cottages of the workers when vacated are snapped up at inflated prices for use as holiday or retirement homes by outsiders seeking refuge from the pressures of urban life, with the unfortunate consequence that young local couples, born and brought up in the area are unable to compete and reluctantly are forced to tear up their roots and seek employment and accommodation away from their natural habitat. The situation is becoming reminiscent of the Highland Clearances, the newcomers not being sheep but strangers who know nothing of the customs and traditions of the valley, do not speak the same language and take little part in the social life. Langdale is turning cosmopolitan. Tourism is the enemy.

The Langdale Valley

Continuing up the valley from Elterwater, walkers have a pleasant alternative to the busy road, a path leaving the village in the near company of Great Langdale Beck, passing along the base of Lingmoor Fell. Beyond two farms, the pinnacle of Oak Howe Needle may be noticed amongst crags on the left. This path joins the old road at the head of the valley and rejoins the motor road at Dungeon Ghyll New Hotel.

Visitors on wheels have no such choice. They must follow the hard road past the time-share complex and a few hotels to reach the larger village of Chapel Stile. Chapel Stile is the largest village in the valley, having shops to meet local needs, a petrol station, a policeman and a bus service. The cottages are arranged to a triangular plan and at the crux is the parish church of the Holy Trinity. This was built of the native slate in 1857 to replace an earlier chapel. It is so perfectly in tune with the environs that it appears to be hewn out of the living rock.

Further along the roadside is an area of devastation, the debris of an abandoned quarry that in its heyday provided the lifeblood of Chapel Stile. Around a bend there is a sudden and startling confrontation with the Langdale Pikes, now seen at close range, and after a stunned appreciation of the dramatic scene ahead out come the cameras.

The Langdale Pikes from Side Pike

The road sweeps round to the head of the valley in a glorious curve, illustrating Nature's abhorrence of straight lines, and arrives at Dungeon Ghyll, a popular place which is named after a nearby waterfall. The spelling of the Norse word 'gill' as 'ghyll' is a romantic corruption favoured by early visitors and adopted by the Ordnance Survey.

A roadside car park, often filled to capacity, heralds the start of adventure and excitement for a growing army of fellwalkers.

A short lane opposite leads to the New Dungeon Ghyll Hotel, the launching pad for two paths that are being trampled to death by too many boots. One, climbing up to Stickle Tarn, has become a river of sliding stones through overuse and misuse, and has been re-routed. The other, the usual line of approach to Harrison Stickle, the highest of the Pikes, soon comes alongside Dungeon Ghyll Force, a fall of 60 feet half hidden in a narrow ravine; upstream is a higher waterfall not seen from the path and rarely visited.

A short mile further along the road is the old Dungeon Ghyll Hotel, the birthplace of rock-climbing in the valley with a wide selection of crags within convenient reach. Here too is the bus terminus and, as the fells crowd ever closer, the end of Great Langdale. But not quite: two apprentice side valleys, Oxendale and Mickleden, carry on the work of the master by providing further easy access into the mountain barrier ahead.

OXENDALE

Thrusting into the head of Great Langdale is a descending shoulder of Bowfell known as The Band and this effectively divides the upper valley into two distinct sections, each entered and traversed by a path with little change to contours. On the south side of The Band is Oxendale.

Beyond Dungeon Ghyll bus terminus, flat pastures carry a farm access lane to Stool End, nestling amongst trees at the foot of The Band. This is the usual starting point for the ascent of Bowfell by a rising path, which in my day was sketchy and intermittent but has now been worn by boots to the width of a cart track. Oxendale is reached from Stool End by bearing left to come alongside Oxendale Beck which points the way upstream towards the serrated ridge of Crinkle Crags directly ahead and high above. After an easy mile, progress becomes difficult at a meeting of angry waters in a rocky setting: Crinkle Gill leaps down in cascades to join Browney Gill which emerges from a ravine on the left and Hell Gill comes steeply down a long slit in the fellside on the right. Prudent walkers will turn tail here, possibly after a short scramble to see the fine waterfall of Whorneyside Force in Hell Gill and return to Stool End.

The rough craggy fellside bordering Oxendale on the south side is Pike o'Blisco, and it was here that I first became aware that vandals were afoot on the high tops. I often visited the head of Great Langdale, always habitually looking up to see the fine cairn prominently perched on the summit of Pike o'Blisco. One day it was missing; on going up to investigate, I found that after surviving the gales and storms of centuries it had been wantonly thrown down and the stones scattered. I was dismayed, summit cairns representing to me pinnacles of achievement to be respected. I reported this act of sacrilege and appealed for volunteers to rebuild the cairn. This help was readily forthcoming and I was grateful, although the substitute did not quite match the elegance of the original. Similar incidents, profaning the sacred, have since taken place on other summits. Among the growing legions of fellwalkers there are some, a few, who find pleasure in destroying the creations of others. To dedicated fellwalkers, summit cairns are friends to be respected.

Oxendale

Mickleden

MICKLEDEN

Mickleden continues the direction of Great Langdale for two further miles with little change of elevation, to end abruptly at the foot of Rossett Pike. It forms a deep trench watered by Mickleden Beck between the rising Band of Bowfell in the south and the steep flanks of the Langdale Pikes. This is an arresting landscape that contributes to the popularity of Mickleden as an exercise for the cramped legs of motorists from cars parked near the hotels of Dungeon Ghyll. The valley is also the key to more serious expeditions to the Scafell range, Wasdale and Borrowdale, and there are few days in the year when it is not traversed by travellers on foot burdened by heavy rucksacks.

A short rise beyond the old hotel leads to a well-worn path, at first accompanied by a wall and later by the beck as it passes below the uncompromising slopes of Pike o'Stickle and reaches an ancient guidestone. Here a path branches right to climb over Stake Pass into Langstrath, while the main path now inclines left for the Scafells and Wasdale. Valley ramblers should go no further.

I have long had a love-hate relationship with Rossett Gill. It is a narrow watercourse degenerated by overuse into a 1500ft ladder of stones that show no mercy to tired and blistered feet, and yet win affection by opening the way to the highest peaks in Lakeland. I understand that to combat further erosion a rough stairway has been constructed up the gill, a solution to which I cannot agree. Steps are for going upstairs to bed. Man-made steps are an affront to the dignity of mountains and out of place in rugged terrain; in frosty weather when glazed with ice they are dangerous to walkers descending. The way to avoid erosion is to teach walkers to travel in single file on mountain paths and keep strictly to established paths without straying on the verges.

The Lakeland Fells are a soothing balm even on wet days and not at all conducive to bad temper, but one day in Mickleden I really lost my rag when I came upon a young couple having great fun by sending their terrier dog up the fellside to scatter the sheep grazing there; this was a most irresponsible thing to do especially as lambing time was near and the ewes were heavily pregnant. I admonished them severely and all three slunk away with their tails between their legs, probably never to return to the district.

LITTLE LANGDALE

LITTLE LANGDALE IS the shy sister of an extrovert Big Brother who parades his attractions for all to see and demands attention as the overlord of the area west of Ambleside. Lingmoor Fells separates the two valleys, much to the liking of Little Langdale for they have nothing in common and little family contact. The lesser Langdale has not the scenic qualities of her Great namesake, nor his brash commercialism, and prefers to enjoy a contented and undisturbed peace. There is more to life than making money. Little Langdale has got it right.

The valley is usually entered from a dip in the Elterwater–Coniston road near its crossing of the River Brathay, along a pleasant byroad heading west. The river, flowing unseen in a deep channel across fields on the left, here plunges in its greatest waterfall, Colwith Force. Beyond a roadside terrace of cottages, a more open aspect is revealed, a thin scattering of buildings occupying a green hollow backed by the Coniston fells, Wetherlam being the most prominent height in view. The focal point of this little community is the Three Shire Inn, so named because of its proximity to the convergence of the counties of Lancashire, Cumberland and Westmorland at the head of the valley, a distinction removed in 1974 by assimilation into the new county of Cumbria. Past the inn, a side road goes down on the left to the river and a lane upstream leads to a fascinating area of disused quarries, some having carved huge holes in the fellside; others are in the form of underground caverns, a labyrinth not without danger for amateur explorers. A small cave higher up the fell was occupied by a notorious smuggler and distiller of illicit whisky, Lanty Slee; on my last visit, his crude hearth was still intact a century after his passing. Less adventurous pedestrians can cross the small field opposite the quarries to see the most picturesque footbridge in Lakeland, a slender arch constructed of slate from the quarries and built to give the quarrymen a shorter access from their homes. This is Slater's Bridge.

Slater's Bridge

Resuming the valley road near the inn, a short rise leads to a junction with a lane to Elterwater, the road then descending and having an uninterrupted view of the higher reaches of the valley and the fine surround of fells which form an attractive background. Little Langdale Tarn occupies a marshy hollow on the left, the river flowing in and out of it; lacking a wooded shoreline, this is an unattractive sheet of water resembling a large pond and few people will stop. The road hereabouts is very narrow, frustrating to motorists, and confined between walls that prevent walkers from escaping to the verges. To the credit of the highways authorities, they have not sought to widen or improve the road, which retains its primitive dimensions, is in harmony with the rustic environs and is a site museum of the days of Lakeland travel when horses and carts and pedestrians had exclusive right of passage.

As the slopes of Lingmoor Fell recede on the right, a lane branches off to Great Langdale, the mainer road continuing to the last farm, Fell Foot. Formerly there was a gate across the road here which was manned by the farm children who opened it for passing travellers in the hope of a penny reward. Now the gate and the children have gone and the road starts an unimpeded climb to the top of Wrynose Pass where still stands, forlorn and obsolete, the Three Shire Stone.

The Roman invaders of the early centuries AD selected Little Langdale as a convenient route for a section of their road linking their forts at Ravenglass and the head of Windermere. Most of this thoroughfare has been overlaid and has vanished apart from on the steep rise to Wrynose Pass where it can still be traced following a parallel course to the present road. During the last war, this was used as a training ground for tanks and military manoeuvres and was left rutted and potholed, since repaired and resurfaced. The one made by the Romans, where visible, shows no signs of damage by their marching legions or their heavy equipment. Which seems to prove something.

Little Langdale

The entrance to Little Langdale

THE GREENBURN VALLEY

A miners' track leaves the south side of Little Langdale opposite the tarn and rises into the side valley of Greenburn, passing along the base of Wetherlam, a fine mountain of tremendous bulk which was humiliated and ravaged by mining activities, long ceased. Abandoned shafts and levels pierce its flanks with the frequency of a much-used pin cushion – I once counted a hundred surface holes – and the wounds have never healed. The steep northern slope falls 2000 feet from the lofty summit and casts a shadow of mourning over the valley below.

The track leads to the site of the Greenburn Copper Works, another dead enterprise that has left skeleton relics to rot. Where there is death there is sadness, and it is sobering to reflect, standing in these ghostly ruins, that men once laboured here and that they too have gone and are forgotten. There is a more recent graveyard in the valley. During the last war, an aeroplane failed to clear the top of Great Carrs, a high point on the enclosing north ridge, and hurtled over a precipice to a final resting place on the screes below, where its shattered fuselage remains to this day. Greenburn is a place of gloom. There are no habitations, grazing sheep are the only sign of life and movement is restricted to the waters of Greenburn Beck as they dance down the valley to join the River Brathay.

I never met anyone in Greenburn. Even the ghosts have gone.

LANGSTRATH

IT IS A JOY to discover in Lakeland today a valley that has no roads, no cars, no sounds of traffic, no buildings, no commercial enterprises and no crowds. Langstrath is one such. Unlike Greenburn just described, which has the same negative qualities, Langstrath is blessed by the sun, has no sad memories, enjoys the exhilaration and exuberance of a beautiful cascading stream and provides for walkers a journey of delight without hazards and difficulties. I have never found the valley of Langstrath in sullen mood.

Lying south of Borrowdale, the valley is usually entered from Rosthwaite by way of Stonethwaite, and after a lovely mile, at a rocky meeting of waters, Langstrath, thus far hidden, opens on the right as a gateway to pleasure. This is one of the most perfect corners of Lakeland. The confluence where Langstrath Beck joins forces with Greenup Gill is spectacular, the tiered cliffs of Eagle Crag soaring immediately above a memorial bridge and the scanty remains of an ancient bloomery used for the smelting of iron ore.

The confluence is bypassed, a lane from the last cottages in Stonethwaite leading to an upstream footbridge from which a path continues along the east bank of Langstrath Beck. The scenery here is dramatic, the cliffs of Eagle Crag being succeeded by vast scree slopes pouring down from the precipices of Sergeant's Crag, while on the west side of the valley a rising skyline lifts the eyes to the summit of Glaramara. The path goes on up the valley and comes abreast a huge detached boulder, the Blea Rock, also known as Gash Rock; this presents a test of climbing skills beyond the powers of the average walker. The delight of this part of the valley, however, is the beck, writhing and leaping in miniature gorges and providing crystal clear bathing pools free of charge or rules and extending a welcome to all who pass.

Midway along the valley, the path slants up the rising fellside on the left to the Stake Pass, there presenting an unfamiliar skyline of the Langdale Pikes, and descends into Mickleden for Great Langdale. A less orthodox upper exit from Langstrath may be made by continuing alongside the beck up grassy slopes to its source, reaching suddenly and unexpectedly where the broad pedestrian highway linking Langdale and Wasdale crosses the outflow from the dark waters of Angle Tarn with Bowfell towering in the background.

BORROWDALE (*in Cumberland*)

WHEN THE POWERS that be decreed in 1974 that the ancient counties of Cumberland and Westmorland should be combined and augmented by parts of Lancashire and Yorkshire to form the new county of Cumbria, one outcome of the amalgamation was a duplication of place names within the revised boundary. Cumbria now has three Harter Fells, three Grisedales, two Troutbecks, yet another Mosedale to join the many, and a multiplicity of Eagle Crags and Raven Crags. And two Borrowdales, one the well-known and frequented valley that comes down to Keswick from the high mass of the Scafell range, the other the little-known and lonely fold in the hills that drains the wilderness of Shap Fells into the River Lune.

Derwentwater

I have never wavered in my opinion that the Cumberland Borrowdale is the loveliest and most precious valley in Lakeland, a pageant of beauty from end to end. This is still true although much of its pre-war charm has become a casualty, sacrificed to modern demands for easier access and greater tourist facilities. The villain is the motor car. Fragrant verges have been hacked away to provide parking spaces, mature trees have been felled to make drive-in picnic spots and replaced by litter bins, classic viewpoints have been eroded and scraped clear of vegetation, and there is noise where once there was silence. These are but pinpricks in the vast canvas of Borrowdale and its glory is unaffected; more to be lamented is the erosion of its romantic charm, now to be experienced only in early morning and late evening.

In a treasury of recollections of happy days in Borrowdale is the unforgettable winter of 1963–64 when the valley was gripped by snow and a hard frost, unrelenting for three months. Traffic was kept at bay by icy roads and every Sunday I walked alone in a fairyland of glittering jewels under blue skies. The surrounding fells were mantled in virgin white and obviously out of bounds, Derwentwater was frozen from shore to shore and had the awesome stillness of a polar icecap, but I was well content to wander along the lanes and riverside and feast my eyes on the splendours all around. I was nearer heaven that winter than I am ever likely to be.

Taylorgill Force

Borrowdale is watered by the River Derwent, formed at the head of the valley by the fusion of two main tributaries hurrying down from the rugged uplands of the Scafell range. One of these has its birth below the gaunt cliffs of Great End in the silent waters of Sprinkling Tarn, where at the outflow a slender stream is released and scampers gleefully down the fellside, chattering happily and obviously glad to escape from the constrictions of the tarn and free to live a life of its own. Youthful exuberance is short lived, however, and independence lost as it is immersed in the dark depths of Styhead Tarn in the shadow of the towering pyramid of Great Gable. Here, after resting a while, it emerges baptised as Styhead Gill and meanders more decorously to plunge finally as a high waterfall into the confines of Taylor Gill, below which it joins forces with the other feeder. This latter starts as a trickle near the Esk Hause wind shelter and soon enters the deep channel of Ruddy Gill, so named from the red hematite revealed in the rocky bed. Then it turns north into the upper ravine of Grains Gill from whence it issues in cascades between the heights of Seathwaite Fell and Glaramara and passes under the arch of Stockley Bridge to greet its ally from Sprinkling Tarn at the foot of Taylor Gill.

Sooner or later every fellwalker in Lakeland arrives at Stockley Bridge, a gateway giving access to a high crossing of the fells between Borrowdale and Wasdale, and a springboard for the finest mountain expeditions in the district. There are few days in the year when this venerable arch is not crossed by booted and laden pilgrims bound for the shrines of Scafell and Great Gable, often in procession, and it is a welcome landmark on the return from a hard day in the high places. The bridge is also, less happily, the objective of illshod and high-spirited picnic parties who have braved the rigours of the mile-long stony path from their parked cars and for whom it marks the limit of adventure. The setting is picturesque, the simple span leaping across a narrow channel carved by the stream between parapets of naked rock.

The bridge was built primarily for the benefit of the dalesmen and their animals on their way to or from Wasdale by way of Sty Head, the only practicable route and for the passage of sheep to or from their winter pastures in the valley. Earlier this century, the bridge survived a threat of replacement, an insensitive plan to construct a motor road to link the two valleys being opposed by the vociferous opposition of conservationists and mountain lovers as an act of sacrilege, and the idea has never since been revived.

Across the bridge, a well-graded zigzag path originally surmounted the facing slope bound for Sty Head, but unfortunately today only small sections remain in pristine condition, the impatient boots of modern walkers having lacerated the fellside with scars of scree: a sad example of erosion caused by those who have little regard and respect for the orderly progression favoured by the pioneers. Another path branches left to follow the stream on a more direct course for Scafell Pike via Esk Hause.

Stockley Bridge has witnessed many changes since the turn of the century, not all with approval. The quiet years were better.

Stockley Bridge – by A. Wainwright and Derry Brabbs

From the confluence of the two tributaries, the combined waters assume the name of Derwent, and as though aware of their promotion to the status of river and of the responsibilities of maturity, now leave behind the excited behaviour of infancy and flow down the valley with becoming dignity. But not always. There have been times, after prolonged downpours or a rapid thaw of snow on the mountains, when the river has been transformed into a raging torrent, flooding the adjoining pastures to the dimensions of a lake, carrying down boulders and debris in a thunderous roar, smashing walls and uprooting trees and generally leaving a wide area of devastation.

Within a mile, the river passes the first buildings in the valley: the farm and cottages of Seathwaite, a tiny community with an unenviable reputation as the wettest inhabited place in England. This is testified by a hidden rain gauge on a nearby fellside which records an annual average rainfall of 130 inches. The location of this overworked instrument is a secret of the Seathwaite farmer: remote from the tracks of walkers, I once found it by chance during my wanderings.

Seathwaite, for long an isolated outpost with access only by a rough cart track, can no longer be regarded as lonely: since the birth of fellwalking a hundred years ago, there has been an increasing procession through the farmyard without hindrance, even the farm animals are extraordinarily friendly, and when the access was given a tarmac surface the motorists came too, tightly parking their cars along the grass verges outside the farm gate.

Seathwaite, once in a little world of its own with few visitors, has become a pedestrian metropolis. Great days on the fells begin and end here.

Seathwaite

The Borrowdale yews

Through an opening in the farm buildings at Seathwaite, a short lane leads to a bridge over the river and across it, cascading down the steep fellside, is the long white ribbon of Sour Milk Gill. A path climbs steeply alongside, passing an outcrop of rocks, Seathwaite Slabs, where novices in rock-climbing can start their apprenticeship in the sport. The path ascends steeply along the stream to reach the upland valley of Gillercombe, where it may be continued as an alternative route to Great Gable; or, by scrambling up the rough slope to the left, a search may be made for the remarkable Hanging Stone of Base Brown, an immense boulder perched on the rim of a crag and seemingly defying gravity.

Another path across the bridge crosses marshy pastures upriver to enter Taylor Gill, thence going on to Sty Head by a route more interesting than the orthodox climb from Stockley Bridge.

Also across the bridge a path turns downriver and beyond a wall it can be discerned, despite long disuse, climbing the fellside in a series of zigzags to the site of the once-celebrated Borrowdale Lead Mine which, in its heyday, produced plumbago; this was known locally as wad, and the best quality was used in the manufacture of lead pencils at Keswick and elsewhere. Although closed and abandoned in the mid-nineteenth century, there are relics still to be seen: the shafts and adits of the industry are now decayed to a state of collapse and are too dangerous to enter. A sad reminder of the past is a memorial stone dated 1775 and inscribed with the name of John Bankes, the Esquire suggesting that he was the owner or manager of the mine.

Further down the river near the bridge carrying the Seathwaite access are the once-famous Borrowdale yews, the 'fraternal four' described in a poem by Wordsworth. Once standing in proud isolation, these venerable trees are today past their prime and are half-hidden by a coppice wood that has grown around them. Time takes its toll, even for a yew tree.

After a further sylvan half-mile, the Seathwaite road crosses Hause Gill on its way down from Honister Pass to join the Derwent and arrives at a junction with the main valley road near the cluster of buildings forming the hamlet of Seatoller.

193

Seatoller

Lacking a church, chapel, school, inn, post office and general store, Seatoller cannot be classed as a village, but has long been of importance to travellers on foot as a place to get a bite to eat and await a bus to Keswick, and in recent years its facilities have been extended by the provision of a large car and coach park, a telephone box and, to complete its emancipation, public toilets. In the old days, Seatoller controlled a primitive unsurfaced road leading up to Honister Pass and exacted a toll for the use of it, this charge being abandoned when the authorities built a more direct replacement to serve the wagons bringing slate down from Honister Quarry and the wagonettes of Victorian sightseers on popular excursions from Keswick, all such vehicles then being horse drawn. Today, the new road is a race track for mad motorists and the old road, now grass-covered, is the exclusive preserve of walkers.

I remember so well the pleasure and relief I always felt when the little bus that plied between Seatoller and Keswick in the early post-war years came in sight up the road to its terminus: it never failed to appear. The driver was an affable extrovert with a cheerful greeting for all his clients as they boarded and many a wry comment for those dishevelled and weary after a gruelling day on the fells. It was his proud boast that he never left anyone stranded at a bus stop, nor indeed anywhere along his route, the bus being often crowded beyond its capacity, especially on Sunday afternoons in the summer. Seated passengers were exhorted to take others on their laps irrespective of sex and those standing were packed tight like sardines in a tin, unable to move their limbs. He was more concerned with getting everybody in than with collecting their fares and on arrival at his destination at Keswick discharged his cargo of human flesh with a smiling goodbye. They were jolly journeys, if jolly uncomfortable, and I was sad when the local firm was taken over by a large company. The camaraderie went too then: much larger buses were used and regulations strictly enforced. Why do the bad old days always seem the best?

194

From Seatoller a good track, formerly serving quarries, leaves the old and now grassy Honister road and heads north, initially at a high level along the fellside and giving a splendid appraisal of the valley, to arrive at the village of Grange after passing Castle Crag: this is a traffic-free alternative to the road for those who prefer to walk or cannot afford the bus fare. The motor road, preferring to keep to the floor of the valley with the Derwent, has more features of interest, however, and after crossing the river reaches a terrace of cottages known as Mountain View, the mountain in view being Rosthwaite Fell, a spur of Glaramara, directly opposite. A path leaves the road here and rises among trees into the recesses of Combe Gill, which has in its upper reaches the Doves Nest Caves; these are formed by a collapse of rocks on one side, and the formidable cliff of Raven Crag on the other; between them a steep climb through Combe Door ends on the summit of Glaramara. An alternative and easier route to the top is by bearing to the right when clear of the trees and following the wide ridge of Thornythwaite Fell to the top.

THE STONETHWAITE VALLEY

Further along the road, the modest little church of Borrowdale, pristine white, appears in a surround of trees and, in spring, daffodils. Beyond it a no-through lane leads into the short side valley of Stonethwaite to a scene that has resisted change in a changing world and still retains the romantic charm of three centuries ago; the mellowed stones of its buildings and walls blend in perfect harmony with a delightful landscape of pastures and woodlands and colourful fells while a crystal beck provides the musical symphony. The Stonethwaite valley is delightful. Here is an epitome of the Lakeland of long ago, a survivor from the past. Here there is still magic in the air.

Eagle Crag above the Stonethwaite Valley

Rosthwaite

As THE JOURNEY down the valley continues, increased activity on the road heralds the approach to Rosthwaite, a village with a fair claim to be regarded as the capital of Borrowdale. The village is aware of the needs of its visitors, those seeking accommodation having a choice between luxury hotels and humble cottages, a choice severely restricted in the summer season. There is petrol for motorists and a post office-cum-shop where postcards can be sent to friends and family left behind in the towns, and the rucksack filled with goodies for a day's outing on the fells. In appearance, the place has changed little since I first saw it sixty years ago except for the yellow lines along the narrow main street, and its beautiful environment not at all, the close surround of fells having the same beckoning appeal I remember from my early visits. The stream flowing behind the buildings is Stonethwaite Beck on its way to join the Derwent, here wandering leisurely across rich pastures grazed by contented cattle. As dusk falls and the road becomes quiet, Rosthwaite is akin to paradise, a haven of rural peace in a perfect setting.

Rosthwaite is an ideal centre for holidays afoot. All around are lofty fells clamouring for attention and promising adventure, sustained interest and healthy exercise for walkers who accept their invitation, and for those who reach their summits, there are panoramas of great beauty and a satisfying sense of achievement. Nearby, northwards, are Castle Crag and King's How, both of modest altitude yet rewarding climbers with commanding full-length views of the valley. Towering behind the village is the steep and rocky height of Great Crag, with Dock Tarn a jewel set in a purple cushion of heather. A path, fast becoming a pedestrian highway, crosses a low pass to the hamlet of Watendlath. Exhilarating high-level routes lead to Grasmere and Langdale by way of the Stone-thwaite valley, and a steep climb by Rigg Beck opens the way to Dale Head and the Newlands fells.

A fellwalker based on Rosthwaite is a king with many thrones.

Leaving Rosthwaite, the road crosses a flat strath of sheep pastures, the only ground in Borrowdale with an absence of contours, but elevations are soon restored to the immediate landscape, and with dramatic effect, as a narrow defile is entered. Here, on the left, Castle Crag suddenly erupts in a single leap skywards as an unassailable tangle of cliffs and scree and lush vegetation; on the right, the lower slopes of Grange Fell abut so closely and steeply that they have had to be cut away in places to allow a passage for the road. In the constricted space between these two rugged heights, the river and the road are forced into close company and proceed alongside as prisoners to a freedom awaiting ahead. The harshness of this deep ravine, well named the Jaws of Borrowdale, is wondrously softened and transformed into a picture of unsurpassed beauty by a wealth of native trees along the banks of the river and on the fellsides where carpets of heather, gorse and bog myrtle add colour and sweetness to a privileged scene. Many years ago I committed myself to paper with the opinion that the environs of the Jaws formed the loveliest square mile in Lakeland. The road was quiet in those days and did not intrude unduly; today it is noisy and often thronged by unappreciative visitors, but my opinion holds good. The beauty is still there. Here Nature is the supreme artist and planner.

A path leaves the road at the Rosthwaite end of the defile and climbs the steep slope of Grange Fell to the delectable summit of King's How, so named in memory of Edward VII. Here, at a large cairn, is disclosed a lovely view of the lower reaches of Borrowdale, Derwentwater's full expanse being seen aerially and backed by Skiddaw in a glorious composition. The upper part of the valley is also revealed with the towering heights of Scafell and Great Gable forming an exciting skyline beyond. King's How, a mere thousand feet above the valley floor, proves again that although the most far-reaching panoramic views are obtained only from the highest summits, the most beautiful are invariably those seen from lower elevations. The path traverses the top and descends north into the quiet side valley of Troutdale where, after passing below Black Crag and its detached pinnacle, the road may be regained near Grange.

The view from King's How

Upper Borrowdale from Castle Crag

The path from the road to King's How is relatively quiet and unfrequented, but not so the next chance to escape from the busy tarmac, where a short signposted detour leads to one of the most popular sights in Borrowdale: the Bowder Stone. This huge boulder, fallen from the cliffs above, has come to rest delicately balanced on a slender keel, like a stranded ship on a beach: it is 62 feet long, 36 feet high, has a girth of 89 feet and an estimated weight of almost 2000 tons. A stairway invites visitors to the rough top, and through a hole in the keel parties on either side can shake hands.

A path alongside may be followed north as a pleasant bypass to the road, which is rejoined near an abandoned quarry, one of many hereabouts: the debris of these disused workings does not detract from the beauty of the surroundings, a bountiful Nature having garlanded the remains with shrubs and flowers. It is the cars and caravans and coaches parked in their recesses that mar the scene.

A delightful path on the far bank of the river, not accessible from the road except by wading, links New Bridge near Rosthwaite with the old quarry road out of Grange along the base of Castle Crag: this is an excellent alternative to the road, which is screened by trees, but is unfortunately not out of earshot. Midway, in a low crag on the left, may be noticed a double cave, or rather a cave opening with an upper storey. It deserves a look inside. This dark recess, not natural but quarried for slate, was for many years the summer residence of Millican Dalton.

198

Near Grange-in-Borrowdale

Millican Dalton was a man of good education and private means and considered to be an eccentric although I see no eccentricity in a preference to live in the most beautiful part of Lakeland rather than the crowded towns. In other ways he was rather odd, making his own clothes, propelling himself along the river on a raft with a sail and using a bicycle to transport his provisions. He was not a hermit, having many friends amongst the early pioneers of rock-climbing, a sport in which he was proficient; he was always ready to offer his free service as a guide on the fells. The upper storey of the cave, which he called the Attic, was his sleeping quarters. He died in 1947 at the age of eighty, leaving a neat inscription carved on the wall of the cave to express a little of his philosophy: 'Don't waste words or jump to conclusions.'

Castle Crag is a formidable adversary although less than a thousand feet in height. There are paths to the summit – becoming steep and difficult in the later stages – from New Bridge near Rosthwaite and from Grange via Low How, trees and the quarry spoil being a hindrance to progress. The shortest route goes steeply up from the old quarry road on the west side amongst wastes of quarry spoil. The summit is crowned by a well-built round cairn set on an outcrop in which is set a commemorative tablet as a war memorial. The view, as from King's How, is superb, including Derwentwater and Skiddaw to the north and the head of the valley in a ring of mountains to the south.

Grange-in-Borrowdale

The road and the river emerge from the tight grip of the Jaws and enter a gentler landscape side by side to reach a road on the left which crosses a two-arched bridge to the pleasant village of Grange-in-Borrowdale, a name now abbreviated simply to Grange by the Ordnance Survey. It nestles below the steep slopes of Maiden Moor, and visitors are offered a choice of accommodation, a post office, places of refreshment and attractive rambles in an idyllic setting, all the sweeter since a council rubbish tip was closed. The old quarry road, for walkers only, arrives here from Seatoller, and a secondary motor road turns south on an alternative course for Keswick, running high along the slopes of Catbells, passing Manesty where Walpole lived and giving a lovely outlook over Derwentwater.

The main road bypasses Grange and continues down the valley into a zone of palatial hotels and greater sophistication, while the river crosses a marshy flatland to discharge into Derwentwater and lose its identity for the time being. The road passes the entrance to Troutdale and a hotel complex and, with Derwentwater now revealed, passes below the long cliff of Shepherd's Crag which is a favourite climbing ground largely concealed by a screen of trees along the roadside. Then Lodore is reached with its customary throng of pedestrians. At the de luxe hotel here, I was privileged to meet W.A. Poucher at his invitation. I had been a fan of his since his first book of photographs of the Lake District was published in 1940: he was a perfectionist with the camera, and on this occasion, although then in his nineties, his enthusiasm was undiminished: he was returning from three weeks in the Highlands of Scotland with his camera but had not taken a single picture because conditions were never exactly right. He was one of the rare breed to whom second best was not good enough.

The crowds who come to Lodore on foot, in cars and coaches, or across the lake to the nearby boat landing, are not necessarily patrons of the hotel; their interest is usually the wonderful scene immediately behind, where the stream meandering along the Watendlath valley suddenly throws a fit and tumbles down a rocky gorge in a series of leaps and bounds, in spate with a thunderous roar, in times of drought with barely a whimper. These are the Lodore Falls, most impressive after prolonged rain but always spectacular. Some of us can feel poetic on occasion without finding expression in words, but Southey, inspired by the scene, speaks for all in his long poem written early last century. On my first visit before the war, admission to the bridge which is used as a viewing platform was through a turnstile on payment of threepence, and although expenditure of such magnitude would have provided me with three ice creams or a bag of fish and chips, I felt amply rewarded by a feast of natural grandeur.

Lodore Falls

Ashness Bridge

Continuing towards Keswick, the road soon comes alongside Derwentwater, giving lovely glimpses of the lake through a screen of trees, and passes the grounds of Barrow House, one of the four Youth Hostels between Honister and Keswick. In a wooded setting behind the house and falling through a height of 120 feet are the cascades of Barrow Falls. Then a side road to the right branches off on a journey of exquisite charm to the secluded hamlet of Watendlath. Gates, a narrow carriageway with few passing places, and a dead end help to deter wheeled traffic, happily because travellers on foot have little chance to escape from the tarmac.

WATENDLATH

Older readers may remember the benign figure of Vivian Fisher who presided at the first gate across the road above the junction for many years after the war. Rosy cheeked, happy and smiling, he had a friendly greeting for all who came along as he opened the gate for them to pass through in anticipation of a reward, and with true business sense closed it immediately after them although others were approaching. He had a ready conversation and would recite poems or sing songs if requested, and sometimes if not. He was a man attuned to nature, sharing his sandwiches with the many chaffinches who hovered around him and never failing to extol the beauties of Lakeland. Yet I was to discover from Keswick folk that he had a dual personality: off duty he was surly, unsmiling and unfriendly, and on a few occasions when I passed him in the streets of the town he was grim faced and scowling with no hint of recognition although I was one of his regular customers. He was a rare character and the Ashness Gate always seems forlorn after his death.

Watendlath

The Watendlath road, still rising and now unenclosed, next reaches a renowned beauty spot where the rustic structure of Ashness Bridge makes a foreground to a classic landscape of the Vale of Keswick backed by Skiddaw range, perfectly posed for the camera. Upstream from the bridge, in Ashness Gill, is a fine waterfall that deserves a mention, but being hidden from sight in pathless surroundings, never gets it. Across the bridge the road goes on past Ashness Farm to enter Ashness Wood, a habitat of red squirrels, running near the edge of the cliff, with well-trodden viewpoints overlooking Derwentwater, which is seen aerially, and a distant ring of fells. The road emerges from the wood to pass along a deep trench between High Seat and Grange Fell, with Watendlath Beck for company, and reaches its terminus at a picture out of a fairy book. The secluded hamlet was immortalised in the novels of Hugh Walpole as the fictional home of Judith Paris. It is a delicate seventeenth-century museum of rural life, unchanged but impinged upon by the demands of the twentieth century for car parks and catering. A rough spot on the stream below the bridge has the ambitious name of the Devil's Punch Bowl, but this is the only turbulence in a world at peace. Such is Watendlath.

Walkers have a choice of paths at Watendlath: they can cross the high fell to the east and descend to Armboth and Thirlmere; or, as most do, they can cross over to Rosthwaite. There is a longer trek to Blea Tarn on Ullscarf, the source of Watendlath's stream, or they can choose an easy ramble around Watendlath Tarn. Rougher climbs to High Seat, Great Crag and Grange Fell, all nearby, are ladders to heaven.

Motorists tied to their cars have no such option. They must return the way they came to the Borrowdale road.

THE ROAD BECOMES an avenue of trees as Keswick is approached, with enchanting paths branching off to the lakeside, and the extensive Great Wood on the right overtopped by Walla Crag. In more open country beyond, the road passes alongside the abrupt upthrust of Castle Head, a classic viewpoint, and is then diverted on a new route to the town centre to reduce the traffic congestion in the narrow streets.

Keswick has changed since my early visits before the war and I am not a lone voice in saying that the town had a greater appeal in the old days when there were far fewer visitors and a man with a rucksack on his back was an object of curiosity. There were few cars, the usual form of travel was by Ribble bus; the only places of refreshment for those of us not sufficiently affluent to patronise the hotels were the Grey Friars Café and Dalzell's chip shop. On days too wet for the fells, steps gravitated to the photographic galleries of the Abraham Brothers, where the high places were portrayed in magnificent camera studies that have never been surpassed or even equalled. After the war Keswick gradually became too tourist-conscious for my liking: new cafés and gift shops sprouted, car parks were provided and too many of the people who now came were not fellwalkers or admirers of the scenery but ice-cream suckers disgorged from coaches.

Over many years of weekly visits, always by bus, I came to know some of the local characters as well while remaining anonymous myself. There was the Ribble bus inspector Scott, who convinced himself, despite denials, that I was Harry Griffin. And there was Winnie, a waitress at the newly-opened Keswick Restaurant, where I presented myself for a meal every Sunday teatime for six years, never varying my menu: my appearance was the signal for Winnie to call to the kitchen, 'Plaice and chips for one.' Poor Winnie: one week she was missing and later I learned she had died of cancer. Today in summer, Keswick is too crowded for comfort, an immense new car park being quickly filled to capacity, and only in the depths of winter can old timers still sense the magic that brought them to the town so eagerly in days gone by.

But no happenings in Keswick's emergence as a tourist magnet can detract from the glory of the countryside around. The town is exceptionally favoured by its location in a wide strath of verdant pastures and woodlands. It lies within a sheltering circle of mountains and fells draped in tapestries of rich colour, with Derwentwater a glittering jewel in their midst. And standing guard over this precious heritage, as he has done faithfully and proudly since rising from the sea millions of years ago, is dear old Skiddaw.

All who sojourn at Keswick inevitably make the short walk to Friar's Crag, a rocky pine-clad promontory jutting into Derwentwater. The way there passes the boat landing stages, from where motor launches ply around the lake in the summer months on a short voyage of sheer delight, calling at the various landing piers around the lake.

The memorial to John Ruskin in Keswick

Derwentwater: above, *the boat landings and,* below, *evening light on the lake*

Friar's Crag, trodden by processions of visitors every day, is so named from a belief that the Friars of Grange used it as a landing place in the days when Furness Abbey was a landowner in the valley. Be that as it may, the prospect over the lake to the surrounding mountains is of bewitching beauty, of pure enchantment that keeps observers rooted. John Ruskin, whose memorial stone inscribed with his own words stands on a rocky plinth here, considered the view the grandest in the country.

There must be hesitation before questioning the opinions of a man as learned and eminent as Ruskin, but with all due deference I venture to say that the view from Castle Head nearby surpasses even that from Friar's Crag. The path to its bare and rocky top is short and steep, and arrival there upon emerging from a shroud of trees is greeted by the sudden revelation of a scene of such superlative beauty as to seem to be out of this world. From this elevation, Derwentwater is seen to greater advantage than from eye level; this is one of the few lakes with islands and they are well displayed in the broad expanse of water. The surrounding heights too are seen in truer perspective and gain in stature from this viewpoint.

Keswick marks the end of Borrowdale. The River Derwent reasserts its independence at the outlet of the lake and wanders away into the peaceful Vale of Keswick.

The view from Castle Head

206

Newlands Valley

NEWLANDS

SIXTY YEARS HAVE gone by since I first ventured into the valley of Newlands and I still remember the feeling of rare privilege that accompanied my early wanderings there, an awareness repeated on many subsequent visits. I had come from a home skyline of mill chimneys and huge factories, an environment without beauty, and knew no other. I entered Newlands as a wide-eyed Gulliver in a dream, almost unbelieving that the scene ahead could possibly be real. But it was all true. This was no fairyland of the imagination; nor, as I first feared, was I a trespasser in a private domain. On the contrary, the valley beckoned me with an irresistible invitation and I wandered unchallenged and undisturbed in a natural garden of pure delight, near to tears at the sight of such an overwhelming pageant of beauty. The whole bewitching prospect was enveloped in a profound peace broken only by the murmur of streams and the twittering of happy birds. I was often halted in my steps and stood transfixed by new vistas, the like of which I had never seen before nor imagined. Here were no chimney stacks blackened by soot; here above the green carpet was a wonderful surround of peaks arrayed in colours of purple and russet and gold as autumn brought summer to an end; there was even a dusting of snow on the highest crests. I had Newlands to myself on that magic day. I returned home but in my mind's eye saw only Newlands.

The beauty of the valley is not without blemishes. For centuries, in addition to the agricultural interests introduced by the early settlers, men have torn holes in the fellsides to extract the stone needed for their buildings, and have burrowed deep into the ground in search of the more valuable subterranean treasures of lead and copper and even the most precious, gold. These mining activities have long ceased and the workings abandoned for Nature to heal. For the present, these places of honest endeavour remain to be seen, some of them traps for unwary walkers, but I prefer to regard them not as ugly scars but as site museums that form an integral part of Lakeland's history. Newlands is not ashamed of its pockmarks but proud of them.

207

Newlands is a shy valley not displaying its charms to the many passers-by on the busy A66 alongside, the two usual entrances from the villages of Portinscale and Braithwaite on the southern fringe of the Vale of Keswick being half concealed and easily passed unnoticed; in addition, the wooded height of Swinside between them hides the interior. Newlands' secrets are for the discerning few who turn aside and go in search of them. The road from Portinscale skirts the western shore of Derwentwater before turning inland as a leafy avenue to emerge into open countryside at the little colony of Swinside. From here there is the first unrestricted view of the valley ahead, the road then descending to the valley's miniature capital, Stair, and linking with the alternative route from Braithwaite.

The more frequented entrance into Newlands leaves Braithwaite on a road that traverses the full length of the valley and goes on to Buttermere, at first curving around the base of the fell known as Barrow before giving a clear foretaste of the middle reaches as it emerges from a band of trees.

The road straightens along the base of Barrow and soon reaches a large curtain of stones covering the side of the fell from top to bottom. This spillage is the debris of an old lead mine on the ridge above and still not entirely stable after a century of neglect; a barricade of boulders prevents the spoil from encroaching on the roadway.

Evening light on Newlands Valley

STONYCROFT GILL

Beyond Barrow's avalanche of stone, a track, formerly a mine access, leaves the road on the right and contours forward into the next valley of Stonycroft Gill, the road dropping slightly to a bridge over the stream descending the gill. Stonycroft was also once a centre of mining activity and a glance over the parapet reveals artificial water channels cut in the bedrock.

The old mine road may be followed upstream in Stonycroft Gill where it will lead to an abandoned cobalt mine high in the fells. But this brings little reward and it is advisable, when a track joins on the right, to pass with it through the rocky gateway of Barrow Door, leaving behind the abrupt dome of Causey Pike, the kingpin of the landscape hereabouts.

BARROW GILL

A track becoming a lane descends northwards from Barrow Door and offers an easy saunter back to Braithwaite alongside Barrow Gill, the great surprise here being the deep ravine carved by the insignificant stream, or more likely caused by a convulsion of nature in ages past.

Causey Pike

Valley ramblers based on Braithwaite have the opportunity to make a simple three-valley circular walk (Newlands, Stonycroft Gill and Barrow Gill) with little effort, while the more active may reach the heathery expanse of Barrow's summit from Barrow Door and return to the village by a lovely stroll down its northern ridge. Beyond Stonycroft Bridge, a byroad goes down to Stair linking with the road from Portinscale and completing a tour of the lower reaches of the valley.

The middle reaches of the Newlands valley beyond Stair form a quiet sanctuary patterned by a mosaic of meadow, pasture and woodland, and nurtured by the lucid waters of Newlands Beck: this is a place of peaceful repose, unexciting maybe but having glimpses of a tortured landscape ahead as the encroaching fells rise more aggressively to greater heights.

A narrow road, little better than a lane, leaves Stair and rises along the east side of the valley to a tiny concentration of buildings with the ambitious name of Little Town which only considerations of grammar deter me from corrupting to Littlest Town for here is no metropolis but merely a farm and a few cottages. On the slope rising to Catbells from the hamlet are the skeletal remains of the Yewthwaite Mine which, on my last visit, still had open adits and shafts ready to receive careless walkers despite a recent fatality. By continuing up the slope to the ridge above at Hause Gate, there is revealed a glorious out-of-this-world view of Derwentwater far below, a picture of pristine perfection. Heaven must be like this. From Hause Gate springs the long rising ridge of Maiden Moor, a high barrier between Borrowdale, and the upper extremities of Newlands.

At Little Town, there is a first near-sighting of the head of the valley but it is partial only and not readily comprehended because of the complexity of the area when seen from ground level. The valley is closed by the three major heights of Dale Head, Hindscarth and Robinson, the former set well back and the other two thrusting long shoulders of diminishing altitude that effectively confine the low ground into three distinct channels. There is not a single final penetration of the fells, as is usual, but a topographical three-pronged unconformity, clearer on a map than on the ground.

There is no doubt, however, that the logical conclusion of Newlands is the deep trench confined by Maiden Moor and Hindscarth, a fact confirmed by the naming of the descending stream as Newlands Beck and of the terminating height as Dale Head. This is the most rewarding of the final offshoots, having been subjected to much industrial exploitation and still yielding relics of former activity to excite amateur archaeologists with a flair for exploration in places long dead.

Easy access to the upper extremities of Newlands is provided by a distinct track leaving the road near Little Town and persisting up the valley on the east bank of Newlands Beck. This track, originally laid as a mine road, gives a simple promenade and in two miles rounds the pronounced headland of Castlenook, site of a former mine. Soon thereafter it arrives at a final confrontation with the rising cliffs of Dale Head which bar further low progress and effectively bring the valley to an end. The scenery here is spectacular: high on the left, the mile-long escarpment of Eel Crags continues the ridge of Maiden Moor, up on the right are fans of scree fallen from the shattered rim of Hindscarth, and between the two, hostile and intimidating, the rugged and shadowed façade of Dale Head soars in a single leap to the sky. On the ground by the beck are traces of exploratory cuttings and probings, and by crossing the stream and following a rising path on the right, the site of the Dale Head Copper Mines, long closed, is betrayed by vivid splashes of green copper malachite on the crumbling walls.

Left *Upper Newlands*   Below *Looking to Newlands Hause*

Returning down the valley to Little Town from Dale Head, the harsh bordering slopes of Hindscarth repel thoughts of exploration, but towards the end of its declining north ridge, heather takes over from stones. The slender termination of the ridge, Scope End, is pierced by many adits known as the Fan Holes, these giving access to the most famous of the Lakeland mines, the Goldscope. This, the oldest in the district, has been operated for six centuries, German miners assisting in its early development; treasures of lead and copper, silver and gold have been extracted intermittently. Levels were also bored into the ridge from the west side and it is likely that in the honeycomb of underground passages there would be a route through the interior from daylight to daylight. The mine closed last century, not because of a total exhaustion of supplies but because of difficulties of extraction.

Amateur prospectors should keep away. In the interior is a deep shaft; the Goldscope Mine is a dangerous place.

Hindscarth and Scope End

Robinson

LITTLE DALE

The western flank of the Hindscarth ridge plunges steeply into the second of the valley arteries at the head of Newlands, Little Dale, a deep trench closely defined and confined by the similar and parallel ridge descending north from Robinson which terminates below the intake wall in a gradual decline through the farmlands of High Snab and Low High Snab.

Little Dale, carrying the stream of Scope Beck down from the heights, contributed to the Goldscope workings by providing a reservoir, still to be seen in a state of neglect. Access to the valley is by a good path from High Snab, this going down to the stream at a rough section choked by boulders fallen from the crags of Robinson; Scope Beck escapes in leaping waterfalls. Above this impasse, the valley may be followed to an abrupt end at Littledale Edge where the final tedious ascent is rewarded by a fine outlook over the Buttermere fells.

THE BRAITHWAITE TO Buttermere road runs along the western side of Newlands in the lee of sheltering fells, to an exit above the last recess, Keskadale, at the head of the valley. After leaving Stonycroft at the end of that dale, the road rounds the heathery base of Rowling End to a green oasis where Rigg Beck comes down from a rugged hinterland.

213

The valley of Rigg Beck

THE VALLEY OF RIGG BECK

An inviting path leads upstream, soon becoming deeply enclosed between the steep slopes of Ard Crags and Causey Pike and reaching a watershed over which Sail Beck takes on the mantle of companion on a long descent to Buttermere. This route is a pedestrian way par excellence, direct, quiet and foolproof, and is greatly to be preferred to the hard road, which continues up a gentle incline to Keskadale.

KESKADALE

Upon reaching the farm buildings of Keskadale, the road shudders in a sharp rising hairpin bend to easier ground, thereafter ascending gradually, unenclosed and uneventfully along the side of Knott Rigg, but many visitors prefer to survey the scene unfolded ahead: this is of the deep valley of Sail Beck carrying the continuation of the road on a long descent to Buttermere village and an exciting background of fells beyond. Fresh landscapes confirm that the Hause marks the end of Newlands.

After a tour of this lovely valley, visitors may wish to call at the little church on the road to High Snab for a personal thanksgiving and a counting of blessings. We lovers of the Lake District are a very favoured species.

Newlands church

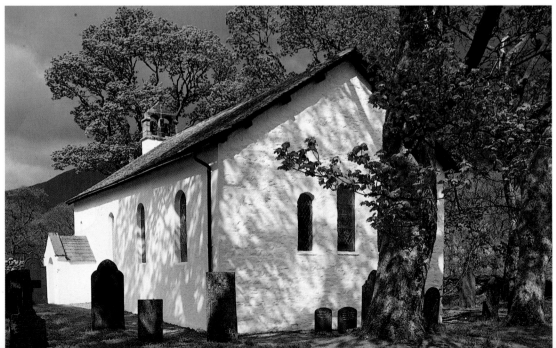

INDEX

Page numbers in **bold** refer to main entries. *Italic* numbers refer to the illustrations.